Anissa Brodon

Invisible

Rebuilding Your Social Life After 40

Index

Index   2
Introduction: Why Do We Feel Invisible?   7
The shifting dynamics of social connections after 40   8
Understanding societal perceptions of age and visibility   10
Personal stories illustrating feelings of invisibility   12
Self-Reflection: Why Do I Feel Invisible?   15
Chapter 1: The Science of Social Connection   19
How social relationships impact mental and physical health   20
The role of aging on our social brain   21
Insights from neuroscience on maintaining friendships   23
Self-Reflection: The Science of Social Connection   27
Chapter 2: Reflecting on Your Social Needs   31
Assessing your current social network   32
Identifying patterns in your social behaviors   33
Defining what meaningful connection means to you   34
Self-Reflection: Reflecting on Your Social Needs   37
Chapter 3: Barriers to Socializing After 40   41

Common obstacles: time constraints, responsibilities, confidence 42
How past experiences shape current relationships 44
Overcoming limiting beliefs and fears about social interactions 46
Self-Reflection: Barriers to Socializing After 40 49

Chapter 4: Rediscovering Your Social Confidence 53
Building self-esteem and managing social anxiety 54
Practical exercises to boost confidence 56
Navigating social rejection with resilience 58
Self-Reflection: Rediscovering My Social Confidence 61

Chapter 5: Rebuilding Old Friendships and Strengthening Bonds 65
Reconnecting authentically with past friends 66
Navigating changed circumstances and interests 68
Strategies for deepening existing relationships 70
Self-Reflection: Rebuilding Old Friendships and Strengthening Bonds 73

Chapter 6: Making New Friends: Practical Strategies 77
Techniques for meeting new people at 40+ 78
Leveraging hobbies and interests to build connections 79

Using technology and social media to enhance your social circle 81
Self-Reflection: Making New Friends – Practical Strategies 85

Chapter 7: The Power of Community 89

Finding and joining communities (local, interest-based, online) 90
Stories of individuals who transformed their lives through community 92
Creating your own community or social group 93
Self-Reflection: The Power of Community 97

Chapter 8: Managing Social Dynamics and Boundaries 101

Understanding healthy boundaries and why they matter 102
Strategies for dealing with difficult social dynamics 104
Balancing intimacy, independence, and group belonging 106
Self-Reflection: Managing Social Dynamics and Boundaries 109

Chapter 9: Social Life Transitions 113

Adapting your social life through major life changes (divorce, retirement, empty nest) 114
Reinventing your identity and roles in social circles 116
Embracing change and leveraging transitions to strengthen connections 118
Self-Reflection: Social Life Transitions 121

Chapter 10: Cultivating Long-Term Social Fulfillment — **125**
Sustaining friendships over time — 126
The habits of socially fulfilled individuals — 128
Continuously evolving your social life to fit your needs — 129
Self-Reflection: Cultivating Long-Term Social Fulfillment — 133
Chapter 11: Becoming Visible Again — **137**
Recap of strategies for rebuilding and maintaining social visibility — 138
Self-Reflection: Becoming Visible Again — 141
Epilogue — **143**
Appendix A — **145**
Resources for further reading — 145
Appendix B — **149**
Worksheets and Self-Assessment Tools — 149
Appendix C: Journal Prompts for Personal Reflection — **151**

Anissa Brodon

Introduction: Why Do We Feel Invisible?

Feeling invisible is a common, yet rarely discussed phenomenon as we move beyond our 40s. It often creeps in quietly—perhaps at a crowded gathering where conversation feels elusive, or when your presence in a room goes unnoticed despite your best efforts. Society subtly shifts its gaze toward younger generations, leaving many to grapple with questions of relevance and visibility.

Several factors converge to create this sense of invisibility. Aging itself brings significant changes—physical, emotional, and social—that alter how we engage with others. Responsibilities such as caring for aging parents, raising teenagers, or coping with career pressures can isolate us, reducing opportunities for meaningful social interactions.

Moreover, societal perceptions around age often reinforce these feelings. Popular culture glorifies youth, subtly sidelining mature adults, contributing to an internalized belief that one's social worth declines over time. Personal stories consistently reveal individuals feeling unseen, unheard, and undervalued, deepening their sense of disconnection.

Yet, acknowledging this invisibility is the first step toward regaining visibility. By understanding why we feel this way, we begin the empowering journey of rebuilding our social lives with intention, resilience, and genuine connection.

Anissa Brodon

The shifting dynamics of social connections after 40

Navigating social relationships after the age of 40 is uniquely complex, marked by notable shifts in priorities, circumstances, and perspectives. The fluid and expansive social networks of youth gradually evolve into more focused, often smaller circles. This natural transition, influenced by life experiences and changing personal goals, reshapes how individuals perceive friendships, professional relationships, and community engagements.

One prominent factor shaping these changes is the evolution of personal values and priorities. In one's 20s and 30s, social interactions often revolve around career networking, shared interests in recreation, or parenting responsibilities. As people enter their 40s, there is frequently a deeper introspection and a stronger desire for authenticity in relationships. Superficial connections become less satisfying, and individuals increasingly seek friendships that offer genuine emotional intimacy, mutual support, and meaningful engagement.

At this stage of life, changes in personal circumstances—such as career shifts, children leaving home, divorces, or relocations—significantly influence social connections. Friends who were once effortlessly accessible through shared activities, schools, or neighborhoods might drift apart, creating social voids. Additionally, the demands of caregiving responsibilities for aging parents can reshape social landscapes, further narrowing opportunities for casual socializing and prompting a reevaluation of relationships.

Moreover, the methods of building and sustaining relationships change notably after 40. The spontaneous, often

Invisible

serendipitous encounters typical of youth and young adulthood become rare. Maintaining social bonds increasingly requires intentional effort and planning. Individuals must consciously dedicate time to nurture connections, often balancing busy schedules and competing demands. This intentionality, though demanding, fosters deeper, more rewarding relationships anchored by mutual understanding and deliberate care.

Technological advances and digital communication platforms also contribute to shifting dynamics. Social media and virtual interactions offer unique ways to maintain existing relationships and forge new ones. While online connections can alleviate feelings of isolation, they often require careful navigation to ensure that digital interactions complement rather than substitute in-person connections.

Another critical aspect involves the shift in friendship criteria. With accumulated life experiences, individuals typically develop clearer boundaries and a more refined understanding of their emotional needs. Friendships after 40 frequently prioritize mutual respect, emotional reciprocity, and supportive consistency over convenience or superficial enjoyment. This emphasis helps foster stronger bonds that significantly enhance emotional well-being and resilience in later life.

Ultimately, navigating social relationships after 40 is about embracing change with intention and openness. It involves acknowledging evolving personal needs and adapting strategies to build authentic connections. By understanding and responding thoughtfully to these shifting dynamics, individuals can create a rich, fulfilling social life that complements their life's second half, filled with meaningful relationships that support personal growth and sustained happiness.

Anissa Brodon

Journal Prompt: Reflect on your current social connections. How have your relationships changed in recent years, and what qualities do you now value most in friendships? What intentional steps can you take to deepen existing connections or form meaningful new ones?

Understanding societal perceptions of age and visibility

As we move through life, we carry the expectation of continually evolving, learning, and growing wiser. Yet, paradoxically, society often sends the opposite message as we age. Particularly after the age of 40, many people—especially women—begin to report feeling increasingly invisible within their social worlds. Understanding why this happens requires an examination of societal perceptions, stereotypes, and cultural narratives around aging.

Historically, many cultures have revered age, wisdom, and experience, placing older adults at the center of social structures. However, contemporary society often prioritizes youth, beauty, and novelty, marginalizing those who no longer fit into these narrowly defined standards. Media portrayals reinforce the value of youthfulness, frequently depicting midlife and older adulthood as periods of decline, rather than growth. This creates a perception that aging inherently diminishes social relevance and worth, pushing people into the shadows of invisibility.

This societal bias manifests in various aspects of daily life. In professional settings, older employees frequently encounter subtle ageism, being overlooked for promotions or seen as less adaptable. Socially, people over 40 may feel dismissed or less valued, as social events and activities are frequently geared towards younger demographics. Marketing and advertising

Invisible

campaigns heavily emphasize youth, creating a cultural narrative that beauty and desirability fade with age, further eroding personal confidence and social visibility.

The consequence of internalizing these societal attitudes can be profound, leading individuals to unconsciously withdraw from social interactions, believing that their value has diminished. Many may start perceiving themselves through the lens of society's bias, exacerbating feelings of isolation and invisibility.

Yet, recognizing these biases can empower individuals to challenge and reshape their own narrative. Visibility after 40 does not have to diminish; it can transform. It involves redefining one's identity beyond societal expectations and stereotypes, focusing instead on personal strengths, achievements, and desires. Communities and social circles that actively celebrate diverse ages and experiences tend to foster environments where visibility is not dependent upon youth, but upon individual value and authenticity.

By understanding and confronting societal perceptions, we can begin the vital work of reclaiming our visibility. Changing these narratives involves open conversations, conscious resistance to age-based stereotypes, and active participation in social groups and communities that value all ages equally. Ultimately, visibility is about acknowledgment, respect, and validation—qualities everyone deserves at every stage of life.

Journal Prompt: Reflect on a recent moment when you felt invisible due to societal attitudes toward your age. What specific societal narratives influenced this experience? How might you reclaim your visibility and reshape this narrative to reflect your true self?

Anissa Brodon

Personal stories illustrating feelings of invisibility

When we discuss invisibility, statistics and broad societal trends can only capture part of the story. To truly grasp the emotional depth and nuance of feeling unseen, we must turn to personal narratives—real-life stories that shed light on the quiet struggles and internal battles many face.

Helen's Story: At 47, Helen found herself navigating the complexities of midlife alone after a difficult divorce. What struck her most was how quickly her social invitations dwindled. Friends once eager to socialize seemed hesitant to include her in couples' gatherings. At events she did attend, she felt disconnected, as if her status as a newly single woman had rendered her invisible. Helen recalls, "I felt like a ghost—physically present but socially transparent. Conversations flowed around me, rarely including me, making me question my worth."

Michael's Experience: Michael, a successful corporate executive, faced abrupt invisibility at age 52 when a younger colleague was promoted to a role he'd worked towards for years. His ideas, once celebrated, were now frequently overlooked or dismissed in meetings. "I went from mentor to spectator overnight," Michael shares. "My years of experience suddenly felt like a burden rather than an asset."

Fatima's Journey: Fatima, a vibrant community volunteer at 60, noticed her contributions becoming increasingly unnoticed. Despite her dedication and innovative ideas, younger organizers subtly pushed her aside, assuming she wouldn't be interested or able to keep up. Fatima expressed, "It felt as though reaching a certain age suddenly made me irrelevant, even though my passion and abilities hadn't changed."

Invisible

These individual accounts highlight the deeply personal pain of feeling unseen, illuminating common threads of exclusion based on societal expectations tied to age. Yet, they also demonstrate resilience. Helen sought new friendships that honored her singlehood, Michael pivoted toward mentoring roles in other contexts, and Fatima founded her own community group, redefining her visibility through leadership.

These stories underscore the universal need to feel acknowledged, respected, and valued. They remind us that overcoming invisibility begins with recognizing our own worth, proactively seeking communities that celebrate all ages, and embracing new paths that reflect our evolving identities.

Journal Prompt: Recall a personal experience where you felt invisible or overlooked. Describe the emotions involved and identify the factors contributing to your invisibility. How might acknowledging this experience empower you to cultivate greater visibility and connection moving forward?

Anissa Brodon

Invisible

Self-Reflection: Why Do I Feel Invisible?

1. **When do I most often feel invisible?**
   Are there specific situations, places, or people that trigger this feeling?

2. **Who do I feel invisible around?**
   Is it with friends, family, colleagues, or in social settings in general?

3. **Do I speak up when I have something to say?**
   If not, what holds me back?

4. **How do I want others to see me?**
   Am I expressing that version of myself openly?

5. **Have I been overlooked in the past in a painful way?**
   Could past experiences still be influencing how I feel today?

6. **What do I do when I feel ignored or unseen?**
   Do I retreat, try harder, get angry, or shut down?

7. **How do I acknowledge myself?**
   Do I validate my own emotions and accomplishments?

8. **Do I believe I deserve attention and recognition?**
   If not, where does that belief come from?

9. **Am I comparing myself to others?**
   Does comparison make me feel less significant?

10. **What does being 'seen' mean to me?**
    Is it about approval, connection, being understood, or something else?

11. **In what ways am I not showing up fully in my life?**
    Is there a part of me I've been hiding from others?

12. **Have I communicated my needs and feelings clearly?**
    Or do I expect others to notice without me saying anything?

13. **What would help me feel more visible and valued?**
    Are there actions I can take or support I can seek?

14. **How do I want to be remembered or known?**
    What qualities or contributions do I want people to associate with me?

15. **If I could speak honestly to someone about this feeling, who would it be?**
    What would I say?

Invisible

Anissa Brodon

Chapter 1: The Science of Social Connection

Humans are inherently social creatures. Our biological, psychological, and emotional well-being deeply depends on forming and maintaining meaningful connections with others. This innate need for social interaction is deeply rooted in our evolutionary history; historically, belonging to a group enhanced survival chances, and today, this remains crucial for emotional resilience and overall health.

Scientific research consistently demonstrates that social connections significantly influence our physical health, mental well-being, and longevity. Studies show that people with robust social ties experience less stress, lower rates of anxiety and depression, improved cardiovascular health, and even increased immunity. Conversely, social isolation has been linked to higher risks of chronic illness, cognitive decline, and shortened lifespan.

At a neurological level, social interactions activate brain regions associated with reward, empathy, and emotional regulation. Our brains are wired to release neurotransmitters like dopamine, serotonin, and oxytocin during positive social exchanges, reinforcing our desire for continued social engagement. This biochemical process highlights how fundamental connection is to our happiness and well-being.

Understanding the science of social connection underscores why nurturing relationships—especially as we age—is not merely beneficial but essential. Recognizing this helps us actively prioritize and maintain our social lives, countering isolation and promoting health and happiness throughout our lifespan.

Anissa Brodon

Journal Prompt: Reflect on your current social connections. How are these relationships impacting your physical and emotional health? What steps can you take today to strengthen your social bonds and improve your well-being?

How social relationships impact mental and physical health

Our relationships profoundly shape every aspect of our lives, influencing not only our emotional landscape but also our physical health. Numerous scientific studies have established the clear connection between social relationships and overall wellness, emphasizing the critical role these interactions play in maintaining both mental and physical health.

Mentally, healthy relationships serve as protective factors against stress, anxiety, and depression. Humans thrive in environments where emotional support, understanding, and empathy are abundant. Close social ties provide an emotional buffer, reducing stress and aiding recovery from life's inevitable challenges. Regular interactions with friends, family, and community members boost feelings of belonging and self-worth, significantly improving psychological resilience.

Physically, the benefits of robust social connections are equally striking. Positive social interactions have been linked to improved cardiovascular health, stronger immune systems, and greater longevity. The presence of supportive relationships can lower blood pressure, reduce inflammation in the body, and even accelerate healing and recovery from illnesses. Conversely, chronic loneliness and social isolation have been associated with increased risks of heart disease, obesity, cognitive decline, and premature death.

Invisible

Research highlights the release of beneficial hormones and neurotransmitters such as oxytocin, serotonin, and dopamine during positive social interactions, which enhance feelings of happiness and reduce the body's stress responses. These biochemical reactions help explain why individuals embedded in supportive social networks often experience superior physical health and vitality.

Understanding this crucial connection prompts us to actively nurture and prioritize our social relationships. Investing in meaningful social bonds isn't merely beneficial—it's essential. By fostering deeper connections and actively engaging with others, we can significantly improve our mental well-being, physical health, and overall quality of life.

Journal Prompt: Consider a time when a social relationship positively impacted your mental or physical health. Reflect on what made this relationship supportive and beneficial. How can you cultivate similar relationships to enhance your well-being moving forward?

The role of aging on our social brain

The brain, much like every other part of our body, undergoes significant changes as we age. These changes don't merely influence cognitive abilities; they profoundly affect how we interact socially and perceive our relationships. Understanding the role aging plays on the social brain can provide valuable insights into maintaining vibrant, fulfilling social lives throughout our later years.

As we age, brain regions responsible for social interaction— such as the prefrontal cortex, amygdala, and hippocampus— experience structural and functional shifts. The prefrontal cortex, vital for social cognition, decision-making, and emotional regulation, often sees reduced volume and connectivity. This can lead to subtle yet significant impacts on our social behavior, including challenges in interpreting social cues or adapting to social nuances.

Interestingly, aging also offers neurological advantages. Older adults often show improved emotional intelligence and empathy, thanks in part to changes in brain function that prioritize emotionally meaningful interactions. Research indicates that while younger individuals might excel in quantity and speed of social processing, older adults typically excel in emotional depth and understanding, often focusing more selectively on meaningful relationships.

The aging brain tends to prioritize emotional satisfaction, shifting focus toward emotionally fulfilling interactions rather than expanding social networks. This phenomenon, known as socioemotional selectivity theory, explains why older individuals might choose quality interactions with close friends and family over broader, more superficial social engagements. This selective focus can enhance emotional well-being, offering psychological and physiological benefits.

Yet, this selective social approach can also increase the risk of isolation if existing relationships weaken or diminish over time. Awareness of these neurological tendencies allows older adults to proactively counteract potential isolation by consciously nurturing both established and new relationships.

By understanding the evolving nature of our social brain, we can better navigate the landscape of aging, embracing changes as opportunities for deeper, more meaningful connections. Emphasizing emotional fulfillment and actively cultivating social interactions can help ensure that our later years are socially vibrant and emotionally enriching.

Journal Prompt: Reflect on how your social interactions have changed as you've aged. Have you noticed shifts toward prioritizing meaningful relationships? How can understanding these changes empower you to create a richer social life moving forward?

Insights from neuroscience on maintaining friendships

Friendships, vital for emotional health and overall well-being, require intentional nurturing—particularly as we age. Neuroscience provides compelling insights into why friendships matter so deeply and offers practical guidance on sustaining these bonds throughout our lives.

Studies reveal that friendships stimulate multiple areas of the brain, particularly those associated with reward and emotional processing. When we interact with friends, our brains release neurotransmitters like dopamine, serotonin, and oxytocin—chemicals responsible for pleasure, happiness, and bonding. These biochemical reactions reinforce our desire for continued interaction, making friendship both emotionally satisfying and biologically rewarding.

Neuroscientific research also emphasizes the role of empathy and mirror neurons in maintaining strong friendships. Mirror neurons enable us to intuitively understand and respond to friends' emotional states, fostering deeper emotional connections. With age, although our brain's capacity for rapidly forming new friendships may diminish slightly, our emotional intelligence and empathetic abilities often grow stronger, providing a neurological foundation for deeper, more meaningful friendships.

However, neuroscience also highlights potential obstacles to maintaining friendships as we age, such as decreased cognitive flexibility or challenges adapting to new social contexts. Awareness of these challenges can empower us to consciously adapt our social behaviors, seeking varied experiences and regularly engaging in mentally stimulating activities with friends to maintain cognitive agility and relational flexibility.

Importantly, neuroscience underscores the necessity of regular social interactions to sustain neural plasticity, the brain's ability to form and reorganize connections. Regular, meaningful interactions help maintain cognitive sharpness, emotional resilience, and overall neurological health, emphasizing the role friendships play in protecting against cognitive decline.

By applying these insights from neuroscience, we can actively prioritize friendships through consistent engagement, empathy, and emotional presence. Simple actions like regular communication, shared experiences, and empathetic interactions become tools for neurological health, strengthening both friendships and overall brain function.

Journal Prompt: Reflect on your friendships and the role empathy and regular social engagement play in these relationships. What practical steps can you take to nurture these connections, supported by insights from neuroscience, to maintain strong friendships into the future?

Invisible

Anissa Brodon

Invisible

Self-Reflection: The Science of Social Connection

1. **How do I define a meaningful connection?**
   Is it based on depth, frequency, mutual understanding, or shared experiences?

2. **Do I feel genuinely connected to others in my life?**
   If not, what might be standing in the way?

3. **How often do I experience loneliness, even when I'm not alone?**
   What does that say about the quality of my social bonds?

4. **Am I more energized or drained after spending time with people?**
   What types of social interactions nourish me?

5. **Do I make time to nurture my relationships intentionally?**
   Or do I assume they'll take care of themselves?

6. **How comfortable am I with being vulnerable around others?**
   Do I let people see the real me?

7. **What fears or beliefs might be limiting my ability to connect?**
   (e.g., fear of rejection, belief that I'm a burden, etc.)

8. **How does technology affect my sense of connection?**
   Do my online interactions add to or take away from real closeness?

9. **What role does empathy play in my relationships?**
   Am I good at putting myself in others' shoes?

10. **Do I feel seen, heard, and valued in my relationships?**
    If not, how might I communicate this need?

11. **What small acts of kindness or presence can I offer to deepen connection?**
    Am I intentional in showing I care?

12. **How has my early upbringing shaped my view of relationships and connection?**
    Are there patterns I notice?

13. **How does stress or emotional overload impact my social behavior?**
    Do I withdraw, lash out, or reach out?

14. **What are my attachment tendencies—secure, anxious, avoidant?**
    How do they influence how I form or maintain connections?

15. **What does a connected, supported version of my life look like?**
    What steps could I take to move toward that vision?

Invisible

Anissa Brodon

Chapter 2: Reflecting on Your Social Needs

Understanding and addressing your social needs is foundational to rebuilding and enriching your social life, especially after significant life changes or transitions, such as entering midlife. Each person's social needs vary greatly, influenced by personality, experiences, and individual circumstances. Reflecting on your specific needs helps clarify what types of relationships and interactions will be most fulfilling for you.

This reflective process begins by asking yourself essential questions: What brings you joy and fulfillment in social interactions? Do you feel energized by large gatherings, or do you prefer intimate, deep conversations? Are you seeking emotional support, intellectual stimulation, or shared activities? Your answers will illuminate what your ideal social network might look like.

Recognizing and honoring your social preferences allows you to intentionally cultivate relationships and social environments that align with your personal well-being. It provides a clear path forward, guiding you towards meaningful connections that authentically reflect your evolving identity and life stage.

Journal Prompt: Reflect on your current social relationships. Are they meeting your emotional, intellectual, and social needs? Identify any gaps or areas for growth and consider what steps you can take to create a more fulfilling social life.

Anissa Brodon

Assessing your current social network

Evaluating your current social network is essential to understanding how your existing relationships align with your evolving social needs. This assessment involves examining the quality, depth, and diversity of your connections, helping you recognize strengths and pinpoint areas for growth.

Begin by considering the relationships you currently have. Reflect on the individuals in your social circle, noting the emotional support, intellectual stimulation, and companionship they provide. Are these relationships reciprocal, balanced, and fulfilling? Do they enhance your life, or do they drain your emotional and mental energy?

Next, evaluate the diversity of your social interactions. Do your relationships encompass varied perspectives, interests, and experiences? Diverse relationships often foster personal growth and prevent social stagnation. If you notice a lack of diversity, this could be an opportunity to expand your social horizons and seek new connections that enrich your understanding and experiences.

Additionally, assess the frequency and quality of your interactions. Are you consistently engaging in meaningful conversations and activities that align with your social needs? Regular, fulfilling interactions can significantly enhance your emotional well-being and overall satisfaction with your social life.

Finally, be honest about gaps in your network. Identify areas where your needs remain unmet, and use this insight to inform your next steps. Perhaps you need more supportive friendships, intellectually stimulating companions, or connections built around shared activities.

Through this thoughtful assessment, you will gain clarity on the current state of your social connections, enabling you to strategically nurture relationships that genuinely support and enrich your life.

Journal Prompt: Reflect on your current social relationships. Are they meeting your emotional, intellectual, and social needs? Identify any gaps or areas for growth and consider what steps you can take to create a more fulfilling social life.

Identifying patterns in your social behaviors

Understanding your social behaviors and patterns is crucial in building and maintaining meaningful relationships. These patterns, often formed early in life, significantly influence how you interact socially and manage relationships throughout adulthood.

Begin by observing your interactions objectively. Do you consistently initiate contact, or do you typically wait for others to reach out? Are your relationships balanced, or do you find yourself frequently giving more than you receive? Recognizing these tendencies can highlight areas needing adjustment.

Explore your comfort zone in social settings. Are you drawn to familiar environments and relationships, or are you open to new experiences and connections? Reflecting on this helps clarify whether your comfort zone is fostering growth or hindering potential opportunities for meaningful engagement.

Next, consider patterns in how you handle conflict and disagreements. Do you tend to avoid confrontation, quickly compromise, or stand your ground assertively? Understanding these dynamics provides insights into relationship health and your emotional communication style.

Finally, assess your vulnerability and openness within relationships. Do you share your authentic self easily, or are you cautious and guarded? Vulnerability is essential for intimacy and deep connections, making it vital to recognize how open or reserved you are in your relationships.

Identifying and understanding these social behavior patterns enables intentional change. By becoming aware of your habits, you can consciously choose behaviors that nurture fulfilling and balanced relationships, enhancing your overall social well-being.

Journal Prompt: Reflect on recurring patterns in your social behaviors. Which patterns support healthy relationships, and which might be holding you back? How can you consciously modify these patterns to foster deeper, more meaningful connections?

Defining what meaningful connection means to you

Meaningful connection is deeply personal and uniquely defined by individual values, experiences, and expectations. Clearly defining what meaningful relationships look like to you is essential for building satisfying social interactions and networks.

Start by reflecting on the characteristics you most value in your relationships. Consider trust, authenticity, empathy, mutual support, intellectual stimulation, shared interests, and emotional depth. Ask yourself which qualities resonate most profoundly with your current life stage and personal growth.

Evaluate past and present relationships that felt deeply fulfilling. What specific elements made these relationships meaningful? Was it open communication, reliability during challenging times, shared experiences, or perhaps a profound sense of mutual understanding and acceptance?

Next, clarify your personal boundaries and expectations. Meaningful connections respect your emotional limits, support your well-being, and align with your core values. Clearly articulating these boundaries helps create healthier and more respectful relationships.

Finally, recognize that meaningful connections require effort, intention, and reciprocal energy. Actively nurturing relationships that align with your definition of meaningful connection fosters lasting bonds and enhances your emotional and social fulfillment.

Journal Prompt: Describe in detail what meaningful connection looks like and feels like to you. How do these connections enrich your life, and what steps can you take to foster more meaningful relationships moving forward?

Anissa Brodon

Self-Reflection: Reflecting on Your Social Needs

1. **What do I need from my social relationships to feel fulfilled?**
   (e.g., companionship, emotional support, intellectual stimulation, shared values)

2. **Do I prefer a few close relationships or a wide circle of acquaintances?**
   How does this preference show up in my current social life?

3. **Am I currently getting enough social interaction to feel balanced and connected?**
   Or do I often feel overwhelmed or depleted by it?

4. **What types of social settings do I feel most comfortable in?**
   (e.g., one-on-one conversations, group gatherings, structured events)

5. **When was the last time I felt deeply connected to someone?**
   What made that interaction feel so meaningful?

6. **Do I feel comfortable asking for help or support when I need it?**
   Why or why not?

7. **How do I tend to respond when my social needs aren't met?**
   (e.g., do I withdraw, overcompensate, feel resentment, seek new connections?)

8. **Are there people in my life who consistently nourish my social needs?**
   How do I show appreciation for them?

9. **Have my social needs changed over time?**
   What influenced those changes?

10. **Do I spend time with people who make me feel valued and accepted?**
    If not, why am I maintaining those connections?

11. **What boundaries do I need to set to protect my emotional and social well-being?**

12. **Are there aspects of myself I hide in social settings to be accepted?**
    How does that impact my sense of authenticity?

13. **How do I show up for others socially?**
    Am I as present and supportive as I want others to be for me?

14. **What do I need more of in my social life right now?**
    (e.g., laughter, honesty, time together, deeper conversations)

15. **What would it look like to advocate for my social needs without guilt?**
    How can I begin doing that?

Invisible

Anissa Brodon

Chapter 3: Barriers to Socializing After 40

As we navigate life after 40, many of us encounter unexpected obstacles that make forming new social connections increasingly challenging. Unlike the ease of friendships forged in youth—built through school, extracurricular activities, or early career bonds—midlife socializing faces distinct hurdles.

One primary barrier is time—or rather, the scarcity of it. By the time we reach our forties, life is often densely packed with professional responsibilities, family commitments, and the ongoing care of aging parents. These demands leave little room to nurture personal relationships or initiate new ones, creating a sense of isolation or invisibility.

Additionally, social anxieties frequently intensify with age. Many adults become increasingly self-conscious, worrying about judgment, rejection, or simply struggling with initiating conversation. This anxiety can hold us back, causing us to retreat further into comfort zones rather than risk vulnerability in new social settings.

Another significant barrier is shifting social circles. Life transitions—such as divorce, moving to a new city, or children leaving home—can dramatically alter existing friendships. Moving to a new place, especially in midlife, can feel especially isolating. The energy and courage required to rebuild a social network from scratch are significant and often daunting, reinforcing feelings of invisibility and disconnection.

Psychological factors, including the experience of being single after long-term relationships or recovering from a domestic violence situation, present another formidable challenge. Trust issues, trauma responses, and diminished self-worth can profoundly impact one's confidence and ability to connect with others. These psychological scars can create emotional barriers, making social engagement feel overwhelming.

Finally, societal attitudes compound these barriers. There is an unspoken but pervasive stereotype that midlife adults should have stable, fulfilling social lives already established. A stigma surrounds adults without close connections, leading to a reluctance to admit feelings of loneliness or actively seek new connections, fearing we may appear inadequate or unsuccessful.

Understanding these barriers is the first step toward overcoming them. Recognizing that these feelings are common—and surmountable—can empower us to reach out and reconnect, rediscovering our visibility and value in the world.

Common obstacles: time constraints, responsibilities, confidence

In our younger years, socializing often unfolds naturally—our lives seamlessly interwoven through frequent interactions at school, work, and social gatherings. However, beyond the age of 40, a unique set of challenges arises, making meaningful social engagement increasingly difficult. Among the most prevalent obstacles are relentless time constraints, growing responsibilities, and wavering self-confidence.

Time Constraints: The Ultimate Modern Hurdle
Time, once abundant in youth, seems painfully scarce in midlife. Most of us juggle demanding careers, home upkeep, and perhaps caregiving responsibilities for aging parents. Every hour feels stretched thin, allocated to duties and obligations, leaving

Invisible

little space for the leisurely pursuit of new friendships or even maintaining existing ones. Socializing starts to feel like an unaffordable luxury, falling lower on our priority list as we manage packed calendars and overwhelming schedules. Over time, friendships fade, and the thought of rebuilding them becomes daunting. The fear of investing precious hours with no guaranteed return on emotional investment often leads us to withdraw further.

Mounting Responsibilities: An Ever-Growing Weight
Alongside diminishing free time, responsibilities steadily pile up, anchoring us further in isolation. Parenthood, career progression, financial pressures, and caregiving roles intensify after 40, consuming mental, emotional, and physical energy. This continuous juggling act reduces the mental bandwidth required to initiate and maintain new friendships. It's not uncommon for midlife adults to feel guilty taking time for themselves, convinced that leisure or personal connections must wait until responsibilities diminish—a moment that rarely arrives on its own.

Moreover, the persistent expectation to excel in multiple roles simultaneously compounds feelings of exhaustion and burnout. For many, reaching out socially feels like one more duty rather than a pleasurable pursuit. As a result, isolation quietly grows, deepening a sense of invisibility and loneliness.

Confidence: Fragile and Frequently Forgotten
Perhaps the most understated yet impactful barrier is our confidence—or the lack thereof. As we age, self-confidence often becomes increasingly fragile, impacted by life experiences, disappointments, relationship breakdowns, and personal losses. Midlife adults can become self-conscious, doubting their worthiness, attractiveness, or conversational abilities. After years

of emotional setbacks or social rejections, many begin to internalize negative beliefs about their social appeal, leading them to avoid situations that could expose them to further vulnerability.

Moreover, society tends to celebrate youth, leaving many adults over 40 feeling overlooked or less interesting. For some, these quiet assumptions erode self-esteem, triggering withdrawal into the safety of familiar solitude rather than risking discomfort or rejection.

Reclaiming Your Visibility
Identifying these obstacles—time constraints, overwhelming responsibilities, and diminished confidence—is a crucial first step toward overcoming them. Awareness provides clarity, allowing us to confront each barrier directly and strategically. By reshaping our priorities to include social engagement, granting ourselves permission to invest in personal connections, and addressing our confidence challenges, we begin the transformative journey back toward visibility and fulfillment.

Remember, isolation is not an inevitability of midlife—it's merely a temporary state. By intentionally recognizing and addressing the barriers in our path, we pave the way toward richer, more vibrant social lives, reclaiming our rightful visibility and sense of belonging in the world around us.

How past experiences shape current relationships

Our current relationships are often deeply influenced by our past experiences. Every interaction, whether positive or negative, leaves an imprint that affects how we perceive, approach, and maintain connections later in life. Understanding this impact is

Invisible

essential in navigating relationships, particularly as we age and strive to build meaningful bonds.

Past experiences, especially those involving rejection, betrayal, or emotional neglect, can profoundly influence our ability to trust others. A single negative event, such as a significant breakup, divorce, or betrayal by a close friend, can lead to guardedness and suspicion in future interactions. We subconsciously erect emotional barriers designed to protect ourselves from repeating painful experiences, often at the expense of fully experiencing new, positive connections.

Conversely, early positive relational experiences can lead to healthy patterns of attachment and communication. Individuals who experienced secure, supportive relationships during formative years tend to carry forward skills that enhance their adult relationships, such as effective communication, empathy, and resilience in conflict resolution.

However, unresolved trauma or adverse experiences from childhood or early adulthood can cast a long shadow over present relationships. Adults who experienced neglect, abuse, or emotionally unavailable caregivers may find themselves struggling with attachment issues, either becoming overly dependent or excessively avoidant. These attachment styles can cause repeated relationship challenges, often without the individual's conscious awareness of their root causes.

Moreover, past experiences influence our relationship expectations. Someone repeatedly subjected to criticism might constantly seek validation, while those accustomed to abandonment may anticipate rejection, even in stable relationships. These deeply ingrained expectations can distort perceptions, leading to misunderstandings, conflicts, and unnecessary emotional distress.

Recognizing the impact of our past experiences is the first step toward healthier relational patterns. By bringing awareness to these influences, we gain the power to address unresolved emotions, reframe our perceptions, and intentionally foster healthier, more fulfilling relationships. Healing past wounds and consciously developing new relational patterns can dramatically enhance the quality of our present and future connections, enabling us to embrace relationships with openness and confidence.

Overcoming limiting beliefs and fears about social interactions

Limiting beliefs and fears about social interactions can significantly inhibit our capacity to form meaningful connections. These internalized thoughts and anxieties, often developed over time, create invisible barriers that prevent us from fully engaging in social situations, ultimately contributing to isolation and loneliness.

Common limiting beliefs include thoughts such as "I'm not interesting enough," "People won't like me," or "I'm too old to make new friends." These beliefs, though typically unfounded, can become deeply ingrained, shaping our behaviors and restricting our willingness to engage socially. Similarly, fears of rejection, judgment, or embarrassment can dominate our thoughts, deterring us from taking the initiative to connect with others.

Overcoming these limiting beliefs and fears begins with awareness and reflection. By identifying and acknowledging these negative thought patterns, we gain the opportunity to challenge and reframe them. Ask yourself if these beliefs are genuinely based on reality or if they are exaggerated fears stemming from past experiences or insecurities.

Practicing self-compassion is another critical step in overcoming these barriers. Recognizing that everyone has insecurities and anxieties can help alleviate the pressure of perfection and reduce feelings of isolation. Allow yourself the grace to be imperfect, vulnerable, and authentic—qualities that genuinely attract and build meaningful connections.

Gradually stepping outside your comfort zone is also vital. Start with manageable social interactions, such as brief conversations or small gatherings, gradually increasing your exposure to more complex social scenarios. Each small success builds confidence, proving to yourself that your fears were less grounded in reality than you initially thought.

Additionally, seeking professional support or guidance through therapy or coaching can provide personalized strategies to manage anxiety, build self-esteem, and develop social skills. Therapy, in particular, can offer insights into the origins of limiting beliefs, equipping you with tools to overcome past traumas and cultivate healthier thought patterns.

Remember, social connections enrich our lives, enhancing our emotional well-being and overall happiness. Consciously confronting and addressing your limiting beliefs and fears can lead to more fulfilling, authentic, and rewarding relationships. With patience and intention, you can reclaim your social confidence and experience the joy and connection you deserve.

Anissa Brodon

Self-Reflection: Barriers to Socializing After 40

1. **How has my social life changed compared to my 20s or 30s?**
   What do I miss, and what do I appreciate about the change?

2. **What beliefs do I hold about making friends or socializing at this stage of life?**
   (e.g., "It's too late," "People are already settled," "I'm too busy")

3. **Do I feel self-conscious or hesitant when meeting new people?**
   What fears or insecurities might be behind that?

4. **What role does my current lifestyle (career, parenting, caregiving) play in my ability to socialize?**

5. **Have past experiences of rejection or social hurt made me more cautious now?**
   How do those memories still affect me?

6. **Do I feel pressure to have it all figured out by this age—and does that keep me from being vulnerable or open?**

7. **Have I unintentionally let certain friendships fade?**
   Why, and how do I feel about that now?

8. **How do my energy levels or health influence my social motivation?**
   What do I need to feel more energized to connect?

9. **Do I rely mostly on digital communication now?**
   Is it fulfilling, or do I crave more in-person connection?

10. **Am I making space for new people in my life—or am I unintentionally closed off?**

11. **What does my ideal social life look like now?**
    Is it realistic given my current priorities and responsibilities?

12. **What activities or environments naturally help me connect with others?**
    Am I engaging in them often enough?

13. **Do I feel guilt or selfishness when prioritizing social time for myself?**
    Where does that belief come from?

14. **Am I waiting for others to reach out first?**
    What would it take for me to take the lead more often?

15. **What one small step can I take this week to nurture or grow a social connection?**

Invisible

Anissa Brodon

Chapter 4: Rediscovering Your Social Confidence

Social confidence isn't something you're either born with or forever without—it's a skill that can be cultivated and rediscovered at any stage of life. As adults, particularly those over 40, many of us experience periods where we lose our social confidence due to changes in life circumstances, diminished self-esteem, or prolonged social isolation. Yet, rediscovering this confidence is entirely possible and deeply rewarding.

The first step in rediscovering your social confidence is understanding that it fluctuates and can be rebuilt through intentional practice. Reflect on your past successes in social situations. Recalling instances when you felt socially adept or enjoyed engaging with others can provide a powerful reminder of your innate capabilities. Positive memories reinforce the belief that social confidence is attainable once more.

Next, challenge your internal dialogue. Negative self-talk, often stemming from past disappointments or insecurities, can greatly hinder your ability to confidently interact with others. Replace self-critical thoughts with affirmations that recognize your worth and social value. Statements like "I have something meaningful to offer," or "People enjoy connecting with me," can slowly shift your mindset, enhancing your willingness to engage socially.

Taking small, manageable steps toward socializing can significantly help rebuild your confidence. Begin with low-pressure environments or situations, such as informal coffee meetups, hobby groups, or casual interactions with acquaintances. These settings provide opportunities to practice social skills without overwhelming pressure, gradually building your comfort and confidence.

Additionally, building your social confidence involves honing your listening and conversational skills. Showing genuine interest in others, asking thoughtful questions, and actively listening conveys sincerity and engagement. By focusing less on impressing others and more on authentic connection, you'll naturally feel more at ease and confident during interactions.

Finally, cultivate patience and resilience. Rediscovering social confidence doesn't happen overnight, and occasional setbacks are normal. Treat each interaction as a learning opportunity rather than a test of your worth. With perseverance and a willingness to grow, you'll soon find yourself feeling more confident and fulfilled in social situations.

Remember, social confidence is within your reach, waiting to be reclaimed. Embrace the process, practice consistently, and soon you'll experience renewed confidence and genuine joy in connecting with others.

Building self-esteem and managing social anxiety

Building self-esteem and managing social anxiety are integral components of improving your ability to connect with others, particularly later in life. Both self-esteem and social anxiety deeply impact your social interactions and overall emotional well-being.

To build self-esteem, it is essential to practice self-acceptance and appreciation. Begin by recognizing and celebrating your strengths and accomplishments, no matter how small they may

Invisible

seem. Journaling regularly about positive aspects of yourself or maintaining a gratitude diary can help shift your focus from perceived inadequacies to genuine appreciation of your unique qualities and achievements.

Another powerful strategy for boosting self-esteem is setting and achieving small, attainable goals. Each completed goal, even minor, reinforces your belief in your abilities and worthiness, gradually enhancing self-confidence. Celebrate each success, no matter how insignificant it may initially appear, to reinforce positive self-perception.

Managing social anxiety involves gradually exposing yourself to social situations in a controlled and supportive manner. Start small, perhaps with one-on-one interactions or structured group activities with clear objectives. Using calming techniques such as deep breathing, mindfulness, or grounding exercises can significantly reduce anxiety symptoms in these situations.

Cognitive-behavioral techniques are particularly effective in addressing social anxiety. Challenge negative thoughts and replace them with realistic, constructive perspectives. For instance, if you catch yourself thinking, "They won't like me," shift this thought to, "I have valuable insights and experiences to share."

It can also be helpful to practice and prepare for social interactions. Role-playing or rehearsing conversations beforehand can help build your confidence and reduce anxiety about potential awkwardness or uncertainty.

Finally, seeking support from professionals or trusted individuals can provide additional resources and reassurance. Therapists can offer structured guidance, tailored strategies, and emotional support to help you effectively manage social anxiety and rebuild self-esteem.

Building self-esteem and managing social anxiety require time and effort, but the rewards are profound. With consistent practice and self-compassion, you will find yourself more comfortable, confident, and authentically connected to those around you.

Practical exercises to boost confidence

Boosting social confidence requires intentional practice and action. The following practical exercises can help you gradually build confidence, reduce anxiety, and enhance your social interactions:

1. **Mirror Affirmations:** Begin your day by looking into the mirror and affirming positive beliefs about yourself, such as "I am confident and worthy of connection," or "I handle social situations calmly and effectively." Repeating affirmations daily helps internalize positive self-beliefs and sets a constructive tone for social interactions.
2. **Daily Small Talk Challenge:** Engage in brief conversations with strangers or acquaintances daily. These conversations can be as simple as greeting your neighbor, complimenting a cashier, or asking a colleague about their weekend. The goal is to build comfort and familiarity with casual interactions, gradually increasing your confidence.
3. **Role-Playing:** Practice specific scenarios that cause anxiety by role-playing with a friend or family member. For instance, rehearse initiating conversations, attending social gatherings, or handling conflict. Role-playing

reduces uncertainty and prepares you for real-life interactions, making them feel less daunting.

4. **Social Journaling:** Maintain a social interaction journal, documenting your experiences, feelings, successes, and challenges. Reflecting on your interactions helps identify patterns, build self-awareness, and track progress over time, reinforcing your social growth.
5. **Visualization Exercises:** Regularly visualize yourself confidently engaging in social situations. Imagine interactions in detail—your posture, tone, responses, and positive outcomes. Visualization can significantly reduce anxiety and mentally prepare you for real-world interactions.
6. **Attend Group Activities:** Join hobby groups, classes, or clubs aligned with your interests. Participating in structured activities allows you to practice socializing in a supportive, low-pressure environment. Sharing common interests naturally fosters connections and boosts your confidence.
7. **Practice Mindfulness and Grounding Techniques:** Before entering social situations, practice mindfulness exercises such as deep breathing, grounding through the senses, or brief meditation. These techniques calm nerves, center your focus, and enhance presence during interactions.
8. **Set Realistic Social Goals:** Define clear, achievable social goals weekly, such as attending one social event, initiating three conversations, or reconnecting with an old friend. Completing these goals builds momentum, reinforcing your ability to handle social interactions successfully.

Incorporating these practical exercises into your daily routine can gradually transform your social confidence. Remember, each small step taken consistently contributes significantly toward building lasting social self-assurance.

Navigating social rejection with resilience

Social rejection, though painful, is an inevitable part of human interactions. How we handle rejection significantly impacts our emotional well-being and our ability to engage socially in the future. Developing resilience in the face of rejection is essential to maintaining self-esteem and continuing to build meaningful connections.

1. **Acknowledge Your Feelings:** Allow yourself to feel the disappointment or sadness that accompanies rejection. Denying or suppressing emotions can prolong the pain. Instead, recognize these feelings as natural and temporary responses that you can work through constructively.
2. **Practice Self-Compassion:** Respond to rejection with kindness toward yourself. Avoid self-critical thoughts and instead remind yourself that everyone experiences rejection at various points in their lives. Treat yourself with the same empathy and support you would offer a friend facing similar circumstances.
3. **Reframe the Experience:** Shift your perspective by viewing rejection as a learning experience rather than a personal failure. Consider what insights you can gain from the situation, such as areas for personal growth, understanding preferences, or recognizing red flags in relationships or social circles.
4. **Avoid Generalizing:** Resist the urge to generalize one rejection to broader judgments about yourself or your social worth. One person's opinion or a single social interaction does not define your value or predict future

outcomes. Keeping rejection in perspective helps prevent unnecessary self-doubt.
5. **Stay Socially Active:** Resist isolating yourself after experiencing rejection. Continue engaging socially, even if it's initially challenging. Maintaining social activity reinforces the belief that rejection is temporary and does not reflect your overall social competence or desirability.
6. **Seek Support:** Share your experience with trusted friends, family members, or professional counselors who can provide emotional support and practical advice. Discussing rejection openly reduces its emotional weight and provides clarity and encouragement.
7. **Cultivate Resilience Through Mindfulness:** Mindfulness techniques help reduce emotional reactivity and increase emotional resilience. Regular practice of mindfulness meditation, grounding exercises, or mindful breathing can foster calmness and improve your capacity to cope with emotional setbacks like rejection.
8. **Keep Moving Forward:** Remain committed to your personal and social goals despite rejection. Remember, resilience is about bouncing back and continuing to pursue your objectives, learning and growing with each experience.

By adopting these strategies, you'll enhance your ability to navigate social rejection constructively. Over time, you'll build emotional strength and resilience, ensuring rejection becomes an opportunity for growth rather than a barrier to connection.

Anissa Brodon

Self-Reflection: Rediscovering My Social Confidence

1. **When in my life did I feel most socially confident?**
   What was different about that time or version of me?

2. **What situations make me feel socially anxious or uncertain now?**
   Are there patterns or triggers I can identify?

3. **Do I focus more on how I'm being perceived or on enjoying the moment?**
   How does that affect my ability to connect?

4. **What positive qualities do I bring into a conversation or group setting?**
   (e.g., warmth, humor, insight, listening skills)

5. **What stories am I telling myself about my social abilities?**
   Are those stories helping or holding me back?

6. **Have I confused being quiet or introverted with being socially inadequate?**
   What strengths come with my natural style?

7. **Do I compare myself to others in social situations?**
   How can I shift from comparison to self-acceptance?

8. **What small social wins have I had recently?**
   Have I given myself credit for them?

9. **How do I recover from awkward or uncomfortable moments?**
   Can I learn to be kinder to myself when they happen?

10. **What environments make me feel most at ease socially?**
    How can I spend more time in those spaces?

11. **Who in my life helps me feel confident and seen?**
    How can I strengthen that relationship?

12. **What does "confident" look like for me now—not just how it used to?**
    How has my version of confidence evolved?

13. **Am I waiting to feel confident before I act—or building confidence through action?**

14. **What outdated labels have I been carrying about myself socially?**
    (e.g., "shy," "awkward," "not interesting") Can I let any of them go?

15. **What would I do or try if I truly believed in my social worth?**
    What's stopping me?

Invisible

Anissa Brodon

Chapter 5: Rebuilding Old Friendships and Strengthening Bonds

Reconnecting with old friends and strengthening existing relationships can significantly enhance our emotional well-being and social satisfaction, especially after periods of isolation or significant life changes. These connections often carry the warmth of shared history, mutual understanding, and comfort that new friendships may take years to establish.

1. **Reach Out with Authenticity:** When reconnecting with old friends, authenticity is crucial. Reach out genuinely, expressing sincere interest and appreciation for your shared past. Simple gestures, such as sending a heartfelt message or making a thoughtful phone call, can reignite old friendships.
2. **Address Past Issues Honestly:** If past misunderstandings or conflicts led to the distancing, approach these topics openly and constructively. Honest conversations can clear unresolved issues, allowing both parties to move forward positively.
3. **Create Shared Experiences:** Plan activities or meetings that foster connection through shared experiences. This can range from casual gatherings or coffee meetups to shared hobbies or interest-based events. Shared experiences create new memories and strengthen emotional bonds.
4. **Be Consistent and Reliable:** Consistency and reliability are foundational in rebuilding trust and closeness. Demonstrating that you are dependable through regular communication and consistent presence helps solidify renewed friendships.

5. **Show Genuine Interest:** Actively listen and express genuine curiosity about your friend's current life experiences, interests, and challenges. Demonstrating sincere interest communicates care and appreciation, deepening your emotional connection.
6. **Express Appreciation:** Openly communicate gratitude for your friendships. Acknowledging the value someone brings into your life reinforces your bond and fosters a deeper emotional connection.
7. **Allow Friendships to Evolve:** Recognize that relationships naturally evolve over time. Embrace these changes rather than expecting friendships to remain as they once were. Flexibility and openness to new dynamics can enrich the friendship.
8. **Prioritize Regular Communication:** Stay connected through regular interactions, even if brief. Simple gestures, such as sending occasional messages, birthday wishes, or arranging periodic catch-ups, help maintain ongoing bonds and mutual support.

Rebuilding old friendships and strengthening existing bonds require effort, patience, and sincerity. By investing intentionally in these relationships, you cultivate supportive, lasting connections that significantly enrich your life.

Reconnecting authentically with past friends

Reconnecting authentically with past friends involves more than simply reaching out; it requires sincerity, vulnerability, and genuine intention. Authentic reconnections bring meaningful relationships back into your life, enhancing emotional fulfillment and providing social support rooted in trust and mutual understanding.

Invisible

1. **Start with Genuine Intentions:** Before reaching out, reflect on why you wish to reconnect. Authentic intentions lay the foundation for genuine interactions, helping you express yourself sincerely and warmly, fostering trust and openness.
2. **Acknowledge the Passage of Time:** Recognize openly that time has passed, and life circumstances may have significantly changed. Acknowledging these changes shows respect and sensitivity, reducing potential awkwardness and paving the way for genuine dialogue.
3. **Show Vulnerability:** Allow yourself to be vulnerable by sharing personal experiences or insights gained during your time apart. Authentic vulnerability encourages deeper emotional connections and invites your friend to reciprocate with openness.
4. **Listen Actively:** Practice active listening by attentively hearing your friend's experiences, feelings, and perspectives without judgment or interruption. Demonstrating empathy and genuine interest strengthens emotional bonds and rebuilds trust.
5. **Offer Genuine Support:** Show authentic care by offering support in meaningful ways, such as listening, providing emotional reassurance, or helping practically if needed. Genuine support demonstrates your commitment and compassion, reinforcing the sincerity of your reconnection.
6. **Be Patient and Respectful:** Understand that reconnection may require patience, as rebuilding trust and familiarity often takes time. Respect your friend's comfort level and pace, allowing the relationship to organically deepen without pressure or expectation.
7. **Share Personal Growth:** Share insights or lessons you've learned from your life experiences openly. Reflecting on personal growth promotes understanding

and can inspire mutual growth, creating stronger bonds based on authenticity and shared maturity.
8. **Celebrate Mutual Interests and Memories:** Revisit shared memories and rediscover mutual interests that initially brought you together. Celebrating these connections fosters joy and nostalgia, reinforcing emotional ties and highlighting the enduring value of your friendship.

Authentic reconnection is deeply rewarding, revitalizing meaningful relationships and enriching your social and emotional life. By approaching these interactions with sincerity, vulnerability, and patience, you can cultivate lasting bonds that stand the test of time.

Navigating changed circumstances and interests

Life is dynamic, and as we move through different stages, our circumstances and interests naturally evolve. These shifts can challenge existing friendships, sometimes causing distance or misunderstandings. Navigating these changes thoughtfully and intentionally can preserve and even strengthen relationships despite differences.

1. **Acknowledge and Accept Changes:** Embrace the reality that personal circumstances, lifestyles, or interests may have diverged over time. Acknowledging and accepting these differences without judgment fosters mutual understanding and reduces friction within friendships.
2. **Open Communication:** Encourage transparent conversations about how your lives and interests have changed. Clear communication prevents assumptions and

Invisible

misunderstandings, allowing friends to appreciate each other's unique journeys and perspectives.

3. **Find Common Ground:** Actively seek shared interests or experiences that remain relevant despite changing circumstances. Common ground, even if limited, can sustain emotional connections and provide opportunities for enjoyable interactions.
4. **Respect Boundaries and Differences:** Respect each other's current lifestyle choices and interests, even when they differ significantly from your own. Mutual respect allows friendships to flourish without pressure to conform or change one's identity.
5. **Be Flexible and Adaptable:** Adapt to new ways of connecting and interacting that accommodate changed circumstances, such as meeting virtually, planning shorter visits, or engaging in activities that suit both parties comfortably.
6. **Celebrate Personal Growth:** View personal evolution as a positive aspect of friendship. Celebrate your friend's achievements, new interests, and life milestones, demonstrating genuine support for their individual growth.
7. **Establish New Traditions:** Develop new routines or traditions that align better with your current circumstances. This can provide a meaningful sense of continuity while accommodating evolving lifestyles and interests.
8. **Maintain Patience and Understanding:** Remain patient and empathetic as friendships evolve. Recognize that some friendships may naturally change in closeness or intensity, but maintaining empathy and openness can help preserve the bond, albeit in a new form.

Navigating friendships through changed circumstances and interests requires flexibility, empathy, and intentional effort. By embracing these changes as opportunities for growth, you can sustain meaningful connections that adapt gracefully through life's inevitable transitions.

Strategies for deepening existing relationships

Deepening existing relationships requires conscious effort, intention, and genuine commitment. Strengthening bonds with those already in your life enhances mutual support, emotional depth, and lasting satisfaction. Consider these effective strategies to deepen and enrich your relationships:

1. **Prioritize Quality Time:** Regularly dedicate time exclusively to nurturing relationships. Quality time, free from distractions, fosters intimacy, deeper conversations, and emotional closeness.
2. **Practice Active Listening:** Develop strong listening skills by genuinely engaging and responding thoughtfully during conversations. Active listening conveys respect and empathy, significantly enhancing connection and trust.
3. **Show Vulnerability:** Share personal thoughts, emotions, and experiences openly. Vulnerability encourages reciprocal openness and deepens emotional intimacy, fostering stronger and more meaningful connections.
4. **Express Gratitude Regularly:** Regularly communicate your appreciation for the people in your life. Simple acknowledgments or heartfelt gestures can profoundly affirm the value of your relationship, reinforcing positive emotional bonds.

5. **Support Personal Goals:** Actively support and encourage each other's personal ambitions and dreams. Genuine support for individual growth demonstrates care, fosters mutual respect, and deepens emotional bonds.
6. **Engage in Meaningful Activities Together:** Participate in activities or projects that hold significance for both parties. Shared experiences create valuable memories and deepen mutual understanding, strengthening your relationship.
7. **Address Conflicts Constructively:** Approach conflicts openly, calmly, and constructively. Effectively resolving disagreements through respectful dialogue reinforces trust, builds resilience, and deepens relationships.
8. **Consistent and Thoughtful Communication:** Maintain consistent communication, even during busy periods. Thoughtful messages or regular check-ins keep emotional connections alive, demonstrating ongoing care and commitment.

Deepening existing relationships involves intentionality, consistency, and genuine engagement. By implementing these strategies, you can cultivate meaningful, lasting relationships that enrich your life profoundly.

Anissa Brodon

Self-Reflection: Rebuilding Old Friendships and Strengthening Bonds

1. **Which old friendships do I miss—and why?**
   What made those connections meaningful to me?

2. **What caused the distance or disconnect in these relationships?**
   Was it time, conflict, life changes, or something else?

3. **Have I taken time to reflect on my role in the distance or breakdown?**
   What would I do differently now?

4. **Is this friendship still aligned with who I am today?**
   Can it evolve in a healthy way that reflects who we both are now?

5. **What am I hoping to gain by reconnecting?**
   Is it closure, reconnection, forgiveness, or companionship?

6. **Am I holding onto resentment, pride, or fear?**
   How might that affect my ability to rebuild the bond?

7. **Have I forgiven them—and myself—for the past?**
   If not, what needs to happen before I can truly move forward?

8. **What kind of communication would feel authentic and respectful when reaching out?**
   Is it a message, a letter, a call?

9. **How would I feel if the other person wasn't ready to reconnect?**
   Can I accept that outcome with peace?

10. **Am I seeking reconnection from a place of love and openness—or from loneliness or regret?**

11. **What values or shared experiences still connect us?**
    Are there mutual interests we can rediscover?

12. **How can I show that I've grown and changed, while honoring who I used to be?**

13. **What boundaries or expectations would make the renewed relationship healthier this time?**

14. **How can I express gratitude, honesty, or vulnerability as we reconnect?**
    What would I want them to know?

15. **What does a stronger bond look like going forward—and what steps can I take to nurture it?**

Invisible

Anissa Brodon

Chapter 6: Making New Friends: Practical Strategies

Building new friendships later in life may initially feel challenging, but it is both achievable and rewarding. Implementing practical strategies can simplify this process and help you establish meaningful new connections:

1. **Engage in Community Activities:** Participate in local groups, clubs, or volunteering opportunities. Engaging regularly with your community naturally introduces you to individuals with shared interests and values.
2. **Leverage Existing Networks:** Utilize your existing social circles—friends, colleagues, and family—to introduce you to potential new friends. Attend gatherings or social events hosted by mutual acquaintances.
3. **Be Approachable and Open:** Maintain open body language, smile frequently, and show genuine interest in others. Your welcoming demeanor can encourage others to initiate conversations and connections.
4. **Take the Initiative:** Actively initiate conversations and invitations to social events or casual meetups. Taking the first step demonstrates openness and interest, significantly increasing your opportunities to connect.
5. **Use Online Platforms:** Explore online platforms and social media networks designed for friendship and shared interests. Virtual communities can facilitate initial connections that later transition into face-to-face friendships.
6. **Attend Workshops or Classes:** Enroll in educational or recreational workshops that align with your interests. Shared learning environments offer structured and comfortable ways to meet new people.

7. **Be Consistent and Patient:** Regularly participate in social opportunities and remain patient as relationships gradually evolve. Friendships often develop incrementally, deepening through consistent interaction and mutual understanding.
8. **Express Genuine Interest and Curiosity:** Show sincere curiosity about others' lives, experiences, and perspectives. Engaging conversations built on authentic interest foster trust and encourage deeper connections.

Making new friends after 40 is entirely attainable through intentional and proactive engagement. By applying these practical strategies, you can successfully build meaningful, supportive friendships that enrich your life and social well-being.

Techniques for meeting new people at 40+

Meeting new people after 40 can feel daunting, but with effective techniques and a proactive mindset, you can comfortably expand your social circle:

1. **Attend Interest-Based Groups:** Join clubs or meet-up groups centered around your hobbies, interests, or passions. Shared interests provide natural conversation starters and a comfortable context for meeting others.
2. **Networking Events:** Participate in professional networking events, conferences, or seminars relevant to your career or interests. Such environments encourage introductions, discussions, and meaningful connections.
3. **Take Up New Activities:** Try new activities or classes you've always wanted to explore. Stepping into new experiences introduces you to diverse groups and offers fresh opportunities for social interaction.

4. **Socialize through Volunteering:** Engage in volunteer work with local organizations or charities. Volunteering not only benefits your community but also connects you with compassionate and socially minded individuals.
5. **Utilize Technology and Apps:** Explore social apps and platforms specifically designed for adults seeking friendships. These platforms can help you comfortably approach new people based on mutual interests or similar life stages.
6. **Participate in Community Events:** Regularly attend community gatherings, festivals, or local events. Frequent attendance increases familiarity with others and naturally facilitates social opportunities.
7. **Become a Regular:** Visit cafes, bookstores, gyms, or other local establishments frequently. Becoming a familiar face makes interactions easier and provides ongoing opportunities for casual conversations.
8. **Approach with Confidence and Openness:** Smile, make eye contact, and demonstrate openness to conversations. Confident yet approachable body language makes others feel comfortable initiating or responding positively to interactions.

By applying these practical techniques, meeting new people after 40 becomes manageable, enjoyable, and rewarding, leading to fulfilling and lasting relationships.

Leveraging hobbies and interests to build connections

Engaging in hobbies and interests is an excellent way to create genuine connections and enrich your social life after 40. Shared activities naturally foster camaraderie and facilitate meaningful interactions. Consider these strategies for leveraging your interests to form deeper connections:

1. **Join Clubs or Groups:** Seek out clubs, workshops, or meet-up groups aligned with your interests. Regular participation provides ample opportunity to meet like-minded individuals and establish friendships based on mutual passions.
2. **Attend Classes and Workshops:** Enroll in classes or workshops that teach skills or hobbies you've always wanted to explore. Structured environments encourage collaboration, conversation, and the natural formation of friendships.
3. **Start a Hobby Group:** If existing groups don't match your interests, consider starting your own. Organizing a hobby-focused group allows you to connect with others who share your enthusiasm and actively shape the social environment you desire.
4. **Participate in Competitions or Events:** Join competitions, tournaments, or community events related to your hobbies. These gatherings often involve teamwork, cooperation, and friendly interactions, helping to build connections quickly.
5. **Host Hobby-Based Gatherings:** Invite acquaintances or friends to casual hobby-related gatherings. Whether it's book clubs, crafting nights, cooking classes, or gardening groups, hosting can create a relaxed atmosphere conducive to deeper bonding.
6. **Collaborate on Projects:** Engage others in hobby-related projects or volunteer activities. Collaborating toward common goals fosters teamwork, trust, and lasting friendships.
7. **Utilize Social Media and Forums:** Connect online through forums, groups, or social media communities

centered on your hobbies. Virtual platforms provide easy access to communities of individuals who share your interests and can lead to real-world friendships.
8. **Explore Shared Experiences:** Plan outings or trips centered around your interests, such as attending concerts, exhibitions, hiking trips, or festivals. Shared experiences create memorable moments and lasting bonds.

Leveraging your hobbies and interests offers meaningful and enjoyable avenues to build and nurture connections, providing fulfillment and companionship in midlife and beyond.

Using technology and social media to enhance your social circle

In today's digital age, technology and social media offer valuable tools for expanding and maintaining your social circle, especially after 40. Leveraging these platforms strategically can significantly enhance your social connections:

1. **Engage in Online Communities:** Participate in social media groups or forums centered around your hobbies, interests, or professional field. These communities provide accessible spaces to connect, exchange ideas, and form meaningful relationships.
2. **Use Friendship Apps:** Explore apps designed specifically for friendship and networking. Platforms like Meetup, Bumble BFF, or Nextdoor facilitate connections with others seeking genuine relationships or shared interests.
3. **Attend Virtual Events:** Participate in virtual webinars, workshops, or social gatherings. Virtual events reduce barriers such as geography or limited availability,

allowing connections with diverse individuals from various locations.
4. **Reconnect via Social Platforms:** Utilize social media to reconnect authentically with past friends or acquaintances. Reaching out through these platforms makes initial conversations less intimidating and helps reestablish connections smoothly.
5. **Share Personal Interests Online:** Regularly share your hobbies, achievements, or interests online. Authentic sharing invites like-minded individuals to interact, creating opportunities for genuine connections based on common interests.
6. **Initiate Conversations Through Direct Messages:** Take the initiative to send personalized messages or comments to individuals whose posts resonate with you. Thoughtful direct interactions often spark deeper conversations and friendships.
7. **Join Professional Networks:** Utilize professional networking sites like LinkedIn to connect with peers, industry professionals, or individuals who share similar professional interests or goals. These networks can lead to professional relationships that transition into personal connections.
8. **Balance Online and Offline Interaction:** Transition online connections into real-world friendships by organizing or attending offline meet-ups and gatherings. Balancing virtual and in-person interactions enriches relationships and creates deeper, more sustainable bonds.

By harnessing technology and social media strategically, you can effectively broaden your social circle, enhance existing connections, and foster meaningful relationships in midlife and beyond.

Invisible

Anissa Brodon

Self-Reflection: Making New Friends – Practical Strategies

1. **What do I truly want from new friendships right now?**
   (e.g., shared hobbies, emotional support, deeper conversations, fun and laughter)

2. **Do I believe it's still possible (and worthwhile) to make new friends at this stage of life?**
   If not, what belief is holding me back?

3. **What environments or activities naturally bring out my most authentic self?**
   How can I place myself in those spaces more often?

4. **Have I been open to invitations or opportunities to meet new people?**
   Or do I tend to say no by default?

5. **Am I waiting for others to initiate—or am I willing to take the first step?**

6. **What qualities do I look for in a new friend?**
   How can I also embody those qualities myself?

7. **What are some common excuses I use to avoid putting myself out there socially?**
   Are those excuses protecting me or limiting me?

8. **How comfortable am I with small talk or meeting new people?**
   What makes me feel more at ease?

9. **What past experiences have shaped the way I approach making new friends?**
   Have they helped or hurt my confidence?

10. **Are there recurring places I already go (gym, classes, work, online groups) where I could engage more intentionally?**

11. **What simple conversation starters or questions could I use to connect with someone new?**

12. **Am I open to building friendships slowly—or do I expect instant connection?**

13. **How can I practice being a good listener and showing genuine curiosity in others?**

14. **What small risk can I take this week to meet someone new or deepen an acquaintance?**

15. **How will I measure success—not by the number of friends, but by how I showed up?**

Invisible

Anissa Brodon

Chapter 7: The Power of Community

Community plays a critical role in enhancing personal well-being, especially in midlife. The feeling of belonging to a community can significantly improve emotional health, provide support, and create a fulfilling social life. Recognizing and nurturing the power of community can transform your experience of connection and social engagement.

1. **Sense of Belonging:** Being part of a community offers a profound sense of belonging and acceptance. Feeling connected to others who share similar values, interests, or experiences combats loneliness and fosters emotional resilience.
2. **Emotional and Practical Support:** Communities often provide both emotional encouragement and practical support. In times of need, a supportive community can offer help, guidance, or simply a listening ear, contributing to your overall well-being.
3. **Shared Experiences and Values:** Communities centered around shared interests or experiences create strong, enduring bonds. Participating in activities and events with others who genuinely understand your perspective fosters meaningful and lasting friendships.
4. **Opportunities for Contribution:** Being actively involved in community initiatives allows you to contribute your skills, experience, and compassion, leading to increased self-worth and purpose. This reciprocal exchange strengthens connections and enhances your sense of personal fulfillment.
5. **Building New Relationships:** Community involvement naturally facilitates new friendships by introducing you to diverse people through gatherings, events, or collaborative projects. These connections

provide a stable and nurturing foundation for a vibrant social life.
6. **Encouraging Personal Growth:** Communities offer numerous opportunities for personal growth through learning, skill-sharing, and collaboration. Engaging with others stimulates intellectual curiosity, promotes personal development, and deepens relational bonds.
7. **Enhancing Mental and Physical Health:** Active community participation has proven health benefits, including reduced stress, improved mental health, and increased physical activity. Regular social interactions within communities contribute positively to overall health and longevity.
8. **Building Resilience and Strength:** Communities serve as sources of strength during challenging times, offering stability, encouragement, and a shared sense of optimism. The collective resilience found within communities can inspire and sustain individuals through life's inevitable difficulties.

Embracing the power of community can transform your social landscape, providing meaningful connections, emotional support, and a sense of purpose. By actively engaging and investing in your community, you enhance not only your social circle but your quality of life.

Finding and joining communities (local, interest-based, online)

Finding the right community can significantly enhance your social life, providing meaningful connections and emotional support. Whether you prefer local groups, interest-based gatherings, or online communities, there are numerous ways to discover and become part of communities that resonate with you.

Invisible

1. **Local Community Centers and Clubs:** Explore local community centers, libraries, or recreational facilities for activities and events. These places often host interest-based clubs, hobby groups, or volunteer opportunities, making it easy to meet new people in your immediate area.
2. **Interest-Based Groups:** Seek out clubs or organizations aligned with your hobbies, passions, or professional interests. Participating in groups that share your interests creates natural opportunities for conversation, connection, and ongoing friendships.
3. **Volunteer Organizations:** Joining local volunteering initiatives provides meaningful ways to connect while contributing positively to your community. Volunteering creates strong social bonds through shared experiences and collective goals.
4. **Networking Events and Workshops:** Attend networking events, seminars, or workshops focused on personal growth, professional development, or specific interests. These structured environments encourage interactions and relationship-building.
5. **Online Communities:** Utilize social media platforms, forums, and online groups tailored to your interests or demographics. Online communities offer convenient ways to connect globally, share insights, seek advice, and establish relationships that can eventually extend into real life.
6. **Meetup Groups:** Engage with platforms such as Meetup, which facilitate interest-based gatherings and local meetups. This is a straightforward and effective way to connect with others who share your interests and goals.
7. **Religious or Spiritual Communities:** Consider joining religious or spiritual groups that align with your

beliefs. Such communities provide emotional support, regular social interaction, and opportunities to participate in collective activities or events.
8. **Educational Classes and Courses:** Enroll in continuing education courses, workshops, or hobby classes. Learning environments naturally foster connections among participants through collaboration, shared experiences, and mutual interests.

By proactively seeking and joining various types of communities—local, interest-based, or online—you can create meaningful social connections, enhance your emotional well-being, and significantly enrich your life.

Stories of individuals who transformed their lives through community

Stories of transformation through community illustrate vividly how powerful social connection can be, inspiring us to seek out and cultivate meaningful relationships. Here are stories of individuals who profoundly changed their lives by engaging deeply with their communities:

1. **Sarah's Journey from Isolation to Connection:** Sarah, recently divorced and new to town, struggled deeply with loneliness. Feeling disconnected, she decided to volunteer at a local food bank. Through volunteering, she not only found purpose but developed close friendships that supported her emotional recovery and restored her confidence.
2. **Michael's Rediscovery Through Interest Groups:** After retirement, Michael experienced a profound sense of isolation. Encouraged by family, he joined a local hiking group, rekindling his passion for nature. His

involvement led to new friendships, regular outdoor adventures, and a renewed zest for life.
3. **Emma's Empowerment via Online Communities:** Facing health challenges, Emma turned to online health forums and support groups. She discovered a community of individuals who provided emotional support, practical advice, and genuine friendship. These virtual connections significantly improved her mental health, empowering her to manage her illness positively.
4. **Raj's Rebuilding Through Education:** Raj, unemployed and experiencing low self-esteem, enrolled in community college courses to gain new skills. The camaraderie and encouragement from classmates and instructors helped him regain self-confidence, leading to new career opportunities and a vibrant social life.
5. **Linda's Renewal in Spiritual Community:** After losing her spouse, Linda felt adrift. She began attending services at a local spiritual community. This new social circle offered emotional healing, friendship, and a strong sense of belonging, helping her navigate grief and find renewed joy and purpose.

These personal stories underscore the transformative power of community. They remind us that by actively engaging with others and embracing community, we can profoundly enhance our lives, overcome challenges, and find enduring happiness.

Creating your own community or social group

Creating your own community or social group empowers you to shape your social environment intentionally and meaningfully. Whether driven by personal interests, shared goals, or a desire for connection, establishing your own group can significantly enhance your sense of belonging and purpose. Here's how you can successfully create and nurture your community:

1. **Define Your Purpose and Vision:** Clearly outline what your community will represent and what its core purpose will be. A well-defined vision attracts like-minded individuals who resonate with your intentions and shared goals.
2. **Identify and Connect with Potential Members:** Reach out to your personal networks, use social media, or participate in local events to identify individuals who might share your interest or vision. Personal invitations or announcements can generate enthusiasm and engagement.
3. **Choose a Suitable Format:** Decide whether your group will meet in person, online, or a combination of both. Consider what format best suits the purpose, convenience, and comfort of potential members.
4. **Plan Regular Activities or Meetings:** Schedule consistent, engaging activities or meetings to build momentum and maintain interest. Regular interactions foster familiarity, deepen relationships, and sustain long-term involvement.
5. **Create a Welcoming Environment:** Ensure your community feels inclusive, welcoming, and safe for all members. Set clear expectations around respect, openness, and mutual support to cultivate trust and positive group dynamics.
6. **Facilitate Open Communication:** Encourage open dialogue and active participation among members. Open communication promotes connection, resolves potential conflicts constructively, and enhances overall group cohesion.
7. **Empower Members to Contribute:** Invite members to take ownership by contributing ideas, leading activities,

or helping manage group logistics. Empowering members fosters a sense of investment, responsibility, and deeper commitment.
8. **Maintain Flexibility and Responsiveness:** Be adaptable and responsive to your group's evolving needs and feedback. Flexibility ensures your community remains relevant, engaging, and supportive for all participants.

Creating your own community or social group can be profoundly rewarding, offering opportunities to foster meaningful connections, share passions, and experience a deeper sense of fulfillment. With thoughtful planning and active engagement, you can build a thriving, supportive community that enriches your life and the lives of others.

Anissa Brodon

Self-Reflection: The Power of Community

1. **What does "community" mean to me personally?**
   Is it based on location, shared interests, values, culture, or something else?

2. **Do I currently feel like I belong to a strong, supportive community?**
   If not, what might be missing?

3. **How has being part of a community helped me grow emotionally, spiritually, or socially?**

4. **What role do I typically play in a community setting?**
   (e.g., leader, supporter, listener, organizer, observer)

5. **When have I felt most connected to others in a group setting?**
   What contributed to that feeling?

6. **Do I allow myself to be seen, heard, and valued within communities?**
   Or do I tend to hold back?

7. **What needs of mine are met through community involvement?**
   (e.g., support, purpose, collaboration, fun)

8. **Have I ever felt excluded from a community?**
   What did I learn from that experience?

9. **How do I contribute to the well-being of the communities I'm part of?**
   Could I be doing more—or perhaps less?

10. **What strengths or resources can I offer to help strengthen a community I care about?**

11. **Am I part of any communities that no longer align with who I am today?**
    Is it time to let go or re-engage in a new way?

12. **How does my sense of community affect my mental health and overall happiness?**

13. **Do I actively seek out community—or do I wait for it to find me?**
    What holds me back from participating more?

14. **What kind of community would I like to build or be part of now?**
    What first step could I take toward that vision?

15. **How can I create a ripple effect—bringing more connection, support, and kindness to those around me?**

Invisible

Anissa Brodon

Chapter 8: Managing Social Dynamics and Boundaries

Effectively managing social dynamics and setting healthy boundaries is essential for maintaining meaningful and fulfilling relationships. As your social interactions grow and evolve, particularly after 40, understanding and navigating these dynamics becomes increasingly crucial. Here's how you can manage social dynamics positively and set clear boundaries:

1. **Identify Your Personal Boundaries:** Clearly define what makes you comfortable or uncomfortable in social situations. Identifying your emotional, physical, and mental boundaries helps protect your well-being and ensures healthier interactions.
2. **Communicate Clearly and Respectfully:** Clearly express your boundaries and expectations with honesty and kindness. Open communication fosters mutual respect and reduces misunderstandings or conflict.
3. **Recognize and Respect Others' Boundaries:** Respecting the boundaries of others is equally important. Being mindful of and responsive to others' comfort levels builds trust, understanding, and stronger connections.
4. **Handle Conflict with Empathy:** Conflict in relationships is inevitable. Approach disagreements calmly, empathetically, and constructively, focusing on finding mutually beneficial solutions rather than assigning blame.
5. **Balance Giving and Receiving:** Healthy relationships thrive on balanced interactions. Ensure that your relationships involve reciprocal support, attention, and respect, preventing resentment or feelings of being overwhelmed.

6. **Manage Social Expectations:** Understand and manage both your own and others' expectations. Being realistic and clear about what you can offer socially helps prevent disappointment and strain on relationships.
7. **Practice Saying "No":** Learn and practice confidently saying "no" when necessary. Declining requests respectfully and assertively protects your time and energy, maintaining healthier, more authentic relationships.
8. **Recognize Toxic Dynamics:** Be aware of unhealthy or toxic relationship dynamics such as manipulation, excessive criticism, or persistent negativity. Recognizing these behaviors allows you to address issues proactively or, if necessary, distance yourself to maintain emotional health.

By consciously managing social dynamics and setting clear boundaries, you can foster more satisfying, authentic, and sustainable relationships. These skills empower you to enjoy positive interactions, deeper connections, and improved overall emotional well-being.

Understanding healthy boundaries and why they matter

Healthy boundaries are essential components of fulfilling relationships and overall emotional well-being. Boundaries clearly define limits regarding what is acceptable behavior from others and yourself, fostering mutual respect, trust, and emotional safety. Here's why healthy boundaries matter and how you can implement them:

1. **Protecting Emotional Health:** Establishing and maintaining healthy boundaries helps protect your emotional health by reducing stress, preventing

resentment, and minimizing emotional exhaustion. Boundaries ensure your needs are respected, allowing for more genuine and positive interactions.
2. **Promoting Mutual Respect:** Clearly defined boundaries promote respect within relationships. When each party understands and respects the other's boundaries, interactions become more considerate, supportive, and fulfilling.
3. **Improving Communication:** Boundaries encourage clear and honest communication. Expressing your needs and limits openly reduces misunderstandings and conflicts, enhancing the quality of your interactions and relationships.
4. **Fostering Authenticity:** Healthy boundaries allow you to express your true feelings and needs confidently. Being genuine about what you can and cannot accept or offer in relationships creates authenticity and deeper connections.
5. **Enhancing Personal Freedom:** Boundaries empower you to make decisions aligned with your personal values and priorities. Setting clear limits provides the freedom to focus on activities and relationships that bring joy and satisfaction, improving your quality of life.
6. **Strengthening Relationships:** Clear and respectful boundaries strengthen relationships by ensuring balanced interactions. Boundaries help establish mutual expectations and prevent unhealthy dependencies, contributing to healthier and more sustainable connections.
7. **Preventing Burnout:** Maintaining healthy boundaries prevents emotional and social burnout by ensuring you have adequate personal space, rest, and time for self-care. Regularly prioritizing your needs supports ongoing emotional resilience and relationship satisfaction.

8. **Empowering Personal Growth:** Healthy boundaries facilitate personal growth by encouraging self-awareness and assertiveness. Setting and maintaining boundaries builds confidence, self-respect, and personal empowerment, enhancing your overall emotional strength.

Understanding and implementing healthy boundaries is critical for cultivating positive, balanced, and lasting relationships. Embracing these boundaries leads to increased emotional security, meaningful interactions, and greater life satisfaction.

Strategies for dealing with difficult social dynamics

Navigating challenging social dynamics is a common yet complex aspect of maintaining healthy relationships. Successfully managing these dynamics requires patience, empathy, and practical strategies designed to address difficult interactions constructively. Here's how you can effectively handle challenging social situations:

1. **Maintain Emotional Composure:** In tense situations, staying calm and composed can prevent escalation. Practice deep breathing, mindfulness, or grounding techniques to maintain clarity and respond thoughtfully rather than react impulsively.
2. **Active Listening and Empathy:** Actively listen to understand the perspective and feelings of others involved. Showing empathy validates emotions and often diffuses tension, opening pathways to meaningful dialogue and resolution.
3. **Set Clear and Firm Boundaries:** Clearly communicate your limits regarding acceptable behavior.

Invisible

Firm, respectful boundaries protect your emotional health and help manage interactions, particularly when dealing with manipulative or overly demanding individuals.

4. **Address Conflicts Directly and Respectfully:** Approach conflicts openly, addressing specific behaviors rather than criticizing the person. Using "I" statements helps convey your feelings without assigning blame, facilitating constructive discussions.
5. **Focus on Solutions, Not Problems:** Shift the conversation toward finding mutual solutions. Concentrating on collaborative problem-solving rather than dwelling on past grievances or conflicts encourages positive outcomes and strengthens relationships.
6. **Know When to Disengage:** Recognize when interactions are becoming unhealthy or unproductive. It's acceptable and sometimes necessary to politely disengage from toxic or harmful situations to preserve your emotional well-being.
7. **Seek Mediation or Support:** In situations where resolution seems difficult, seeking mediation through a neutral third party or professional counseling can help. External support can provide clarity, balance perspectives, and guide interactions toward resolution.
8. **Reflect and Learn:** After difficult interactions, reflect on what occurred and identify areas for personal growth. Learning from these experiences enhances your skills in managing future dynamics, increasing resilience and relational wisdom.

Effectively managing challenging social dynamics fosters healthier, more supportive relationships. By implementing these strategies, you enhance your emotional intelligence, relationship skills, and overall quality of your social interactions.

Anissa Brodon

Balancing intimacy, independence, and group belonging

Achieving balance among intimacy, independence, and group belonging is essential for healthy, fulfilling relationships and personal growth, especially later in life. Each of these elements contributes uniquely to our emotional well-being, and finding harmony among them can significantly enhance the quality of your social life. Here are strategies to maintain this important balance:

1. **Prioritize Personal Space:** Allocate regular time for yourself, respecting your need for independence. Personal space allows for reflection, relaxation, and personal growth, ultimately enriching your contributions to intimate relationships and group interactions.
2. **Cultivate Close Relationships:** Invest intentional effort in maintaining deep connections with close friends or loved ones. Intimacy requires openness, vulnerability, and consistent communication, nurturing bonds that provide emotional support and fulfillment.
3. **Engage in Group Activities:** Regularly participate in community or group activities that align with your interests and values. Group belonging fosters a sense of identity, camaraderie, and mutual support, enhancing your sense of connection and social identity.
4. **Clearly Communicate Your Needs:** Openly express your needs for intimacy, independence, or social connection. Clear communication ensures others understand your boundaries and desires, promoting mutual respect and balance within relationships.
5. **Respect Others' Boundaries:** Recognize and respect the varying needs of your friends, family, and community members. Understanding and accommodating each other's

boundaries and preferences enhances relationship harmony and mutual satisfaction.
6. **Embrace Flexible Roles:** Allow roles and dynamics within relationships to evolve naturally. Flexibility helps balance intimacy and independence, allowing relationships to adapt smoothly through different stages of life and changing personal circumstances.
7. **Practice Mindful Presence:** When engaging with intimate partners, friends, or groups, be fully present and mindful. Mindful interactions deepen emotional connections, increase relational satisfaction, and promote meaningful engagement.
8. **Regularly Reflect and Adjust:** Periodically evaluate the balance among your intimacy, independence, and social belonging. Reflection enables you to recognize imbalances early and adjust your actions or boundaries accordingly, ensuring sustained emotional health and relationship satisfaction.

Balancing intimacy, independence, and group belonging provides a foundation for a rich, well-rounded social life. By actively nurturing each aspect, you create more fulfilling relationships, enhance your personal well-being, and foster lasting emotional satisfaction.

Anissa Brodon

Self-Reflection: Managing Social Dynamics and Boundaries

1. **How do I typically respond to conflict or tension in social settings?**
   Do I address it, avoid it, or internalize it?

2. **Do I feel drained or energized after spending time with certain people?**
   What does that say about the dynamics in those relationships?

3. **What types of behaviors or comments cross a boundary for me?**
   Do I communicate those limits clearly?

4. **Am I more likely to overextend myself to please others, or to withdraw when overwhelmed?**
   Why?

5. **Have I ever stayed in a friendship or group out of guilt, habit, or fear of judgment?**
   What would it look like to choose differently?

6. **Do I feel safe being honest and vulnerable with the people I spend time with?**
   If not, why?

7. **How do I handle being asked for emotional labor or support when I have nothing left to give?**

8. **What boundaries do I currently have in place—and are they being respected?**

9. **Where in my life am I tolerating disrespect, manipulation, or imbalance?**
   What would it take to speak up or step away?

10. **Am I able to say "no" without over-explaining or feeling guilty?**
    How do I react when others set boundaries with me?

11. **Do I notice power dynamics in my social circles?**
    How do those dynamics affect the way I behave or feel?

12. **How do I manage my time between social commitments and personal needs?**
    Is there an imbalance?

13. **Have I confused being "nice" with being boundary-less?**
    How can I reframe assertiveness as self-respect?

14. **What kind of social environment allows me to feel free, respected, and authentic?**

15. **What's one boundary I'd like to set (or strengthen) this week—and how can I do it with clarity and kindness?**

Invisible

Anissa Brodon

Invisible

Chapter 9: Social Life Transitions

Life transitions—such as retirement, moving to a new place, divorce, or children leaving home—often significantly impact our social lives. These changes can alter familiar social patterns and require us to adapt and rebuild connections. Understanding and navigating these transitions proactively can help ensure a supportive and enriching social environment.

1. **Recognizing the Impact of Transitions:** Acknowledge that transitions may initially bring feelings of loss or isolation. Recognizing these emotions as natural can help you process changes more effectively and begin rebuilding your social networks with clarity.
2. **Maintaining Established Connections:** Stay connected to familiar relationships despite changing circumstances. Efforts to maintain regular communication with friends and family provide emotional stability and continuity during transitional periods.
3. **Establishing New Networks:** Actively seek opportunities to create new connections appropriate to your current life stage. Engage in activities or communities that reflect your evolving interests and values.
4. **Embracing Flexibility and Openness:** Approach new relationships and social situations with openness and flexibility. Adaptability allows for the exploration of new experiences and interactions, fostering meaningful connections.
5. **Creating Routines and Rituals:** Establish consistent routines or rituals within your social interactions. Regular gatherings, meetings, or shared activities can provide structure and a sense of belonging, easing the transition into new social contexts.

6. **Seeking Support Networks:** Seek out support groups or communities of individuals experiencing similar transitions. Shared experiences and mutual understanding create strong bonds and facilitate emotional support.
7. **Focusing on Self-Growth:** Utilize transitions as opportunities for personal growth. Engage in activities that develop new skills, hobbies, or interests, enriching your personal life and expanding your social opportunities.
8. **Celebrating New Beginnings:** Embrace transitions as positive opportunities for renewal and transformation. Celebrate new relationships, opportunities, and experiences, fostering an optimistic outlook and vibrant social life.

Effectively navigating social life transitions involves embracing change, maintaining meaningful connections, and proactively building new relationships. By acknowledging transitions as opportunities for growth, you can cultivate a thriving and supportive social environment throughout life's varied chapters.

Adapting your social life through major life changes (divorce, retirement, empty nest)

Significant life changes such as divorce, retirement, or children leaving home (empty nest) can deeply impact your social connections and overall sense of belonging. Each of these transitions involves adjustments in your social networks, emotional expectations, and daily routines. By proactively adapting your social life to these changes, you can emerge stronger and more socially fulfilled.

Invisible

1. **Acknowledging the Change:** Recognize and validate the emotional complexity that comes with major life transitions. Allow yourself to grieve losses, celebrate new possibilities, and give yourself the time needed to adjust socially and emotionally.
2. **Reevaluating Social Needs:** Assess your current social needs and preferences, understanding they may differ significantly after a major transition. Clearly identifying your new social desires and priorities can help you shape meaningful connections moving forward.
3. **Staying Connected to Familiar Networks:** Maintain relationships that provide stability and emotional support during transitional times. Regular contact with trusted friends, family, or colleagues can ease feelings of isolation and offer continuity.
4. **Cultivating New Relationships:** Actively seek out new relationships that align with your changing interests and lifestyle. Engage with new social circles, join clubs, or participate in community events to foster fresh connections.
5. **Exploring New Interests:** Use transitions as an opportunity to explore new hobbies, passions, or volunteer opportunities. Engaging in new activities introduces you to diverse social groups and helps build fulfilling connections around shared interests.
6. **Creating New Routines:** Establish new social routines to fill gaps left by previous life stages. Regular activities such as weekly meet-ups, classes, or social gatherings provide structure and purpose, supporting emotional well-being.
7. **Seeking Supportive Networks:** Consider joining support groups or community networks specific to your transition (such as divorce support groups, retirement

communities, or empty nest forums). These groups offer empathy, practical advice, and a sense of solidarity.
8. **Focusing on Personal Growth:** Embrace transitions as opportunities for personal development. Invest in self-care, self-reflection, and new learning experiences, enabling you to build confidence and social resilience.

Major life transitions, while challenging, also provide valuable opportunities to redefine and enrich your social life. By proactively adapting and embracing these changes, you can create a vibrant and supportive social environment that enhances your emotional and personal growth.

Reinventing your identity and roles in social circles

Major life changes provide not only challenges but also unique opportunities to reinvent your identity and redefine your roles within your social circles. Whether adjusting to retirement, navigating post-divorce life, or adapting to an empty nest, reinventing yourself socially can lead to newfound purpose, meaningful connections, and enhanced self-awareness.

1. **Embracing Change as Opportunity:** View significant transitions as opportunities to explore and redefine who you want to become socially. Adopt an open mindset that welcomes self-discovery and new personal identities aligned with your evolving circumstances.
2. **Self-Reflection and Awareness:** Take time for introspection to understand your current values, desires, and social needs. Identifying what matters most to you now will guide how you redefine your identity within existing and new social circles.

3. **Setting Intentional Goals:** Clearly outline what you wish to achieve socially—whether building deeper friendships, cultivating new relationships, or contributing to your community. Intentional goal-setting provides clarity and motivation for reinventing yourself.
4. **Engaging in New Roles:** Consider taking on new roles or responsibilities within social groups, communities, or volunteer organizations. New roles offer chances to demonstrate different skills and qualities, helping to reshape how others perceive you.
5. **Developing New Interests and Skills:** Actively seek opportunities to learn new skills or pursue fresh interests. These pursuits naturally introduce new social contexts and connections, contributing significantly to your reinvented identity.
6. **Open Communication:** Be open with your existing social circles about your evolving identity and interests. Honest communication allows your friends and community to understand and support your journey, creating stronger, more authentic relationships.
7. **Building Confidence in Your New Identity:** Confidence is essential in embracing and expressing your reinvented identity. Practice self-affirmation, celebrate your progress, and surround yourself with supportive, positive influences.
8. **Allowing Space for Evolving Relationships:** Recognize that as you change, relationships may naturally shift. Allow relationships to evolve, embracing both new connections and existing friendships that grow and adapt alongside your transformation.

Reinventing your identity and roles within social circles is a deeply rewarding process that can lead to a richer, more satisfying social life. Embrace this opportunity with openness and enthusiasm, and you will discover a revitalized sense of self and community.

Embracing change and leveraging transitions to strengthen connections

Major life transitions, while challenging, also provide unique opportunities to deepen and enrich your social relationships. Embracing change proactively can lead to stronger connections, deeper friendships, and a renewed sense of purpose within your social networks.

1. **Recognize Transitions as Catalysts:** View life changes as catalysts for growth and deeper social connections. Understanding that transitions can foster resilience and adaptability helps you approach them with optimism and intentionality.
2. **Communicate Your Journey Openly:** Share your experiences, feelings, and insights openly with trusted friends and family. Authentic communication strengthens emotional bonds and encourages others to support you through periods of change.
3. **Seek and Provide Mutual Support:** Actively seek support from your social circles, while also offering your support to others experiencing similar transitions. Mutual support creates powerful bonds rooted in empathy, compassion, and shared understanding.
4. **Engage in Reflective Conversations:** Initiate meaningful, reflective discussions about life transitions with friends or groups. These conversations often reveal common experiences, fostering deeper emotional connections and community cohesion.
5. **Prioritize Meaningful Connections:** Focus on nurturing relationships that offer emotional depth and

genuine connection. Investing time and emotional energy in these relationships can provide stability and comfort during transitional periods.
6. **Celebrate Milestones Together:** Create opportunities to celebrate significant milestones and achievements together. Shared celebrations reinforce social bonds, validate collective experiences, and provide emotional reinforcement during transitions.
7. **Explore New Shared Interests:** Discover and pursue new shared interests or activities with your social circle during periods of transition. Shared experiences can introduce freshness into relationships, keeping connections vibrant and engaging.
8. **Embrace Flexibility and Openness:** Maintain openness and flexibility in your relationships, allowing them to naturally adapt and evolve alongside your life changes. Embracing adaptability enhances resilience and the capacity to maintain lasting connections.

By consciously embracing change and leveraging transitions, you can significantly strengthen your existing social relationships and build new, meaningful connections. Each transition holds the potential to enrich your social life, enhance your emotional resilience, and deepen your sense of belonging.

Anissa Brodon

Self-Reflection: Social Life Transitions

1. **What major life transition am I currently experiencing—or have recently gone through?**
   (e.g., divorce, becoming an empty nester, moving, job change, retirement)

2. **How has this transition impacted my social life or sense of connection?**

3. **What friendships or relationships have shifted during this time?**
   Are there ones I've outgrown or long to rekindle?

4. **Am I grieving any loss of community, identity, or routine in my social life?**
   Have I given myself space to feel that loss?

5. **Do I feel isolated, uncertain, or liberated in this transition?**
   Maybe a mix of all three?

6. **What did my social life look like before this change—and what do I want it to look like now?**

7. **What relationships have remained steady during this time of change?**
   What makes those connections resilient?

8. **Am I resisting this transition—or leaning into the new possibilities it offers?**
   Why?

9. **What habits or mindsets from my "old life" no longer serve me socially?**
   What am I ready to release?

10. **What are my current social needs, and how have they shifted with this transition?**

11. **What types of people or communities would support the version of me I'm becoming?**

12. **Have I been open with others about what I'm going through?**
    If not, what might help me feel safe to share?

13. **What strengths or skills am I discovering about myself through this social shift?**

14. **What's one small step I can take to rebuild or expand my social world in this new chapter?**

15. **How can I honor both where I've been and where I'm headed socially and emotionally?**

Invisible

Anissa Brodon

Chapter 10: Cultivating Long-Term Social Fulfillment

Cultivating long-term social fulfillment involves consistently nurturing meaningful connections and proactively engaging in activities that enrich your life and the lives of those around you. Sustained social satisfaction is achieved through intentional, ongoing efforts that prioritize relationship health, personal growth, and community involvement.

1. **Investing in Deep Relationships:** Prioritize relationships that offer emotional depth, trust, and mutual support. Regularly invest time and energy into nurturing these bonds to sustain their strength and vitality over the long term.
2. **Continuous Personal Growth:** Embrace lifelong learning and personal development to continually enhance your social skills, emotional intelligence, and self-awareness. Ongoing growth ensures your social interactions remain meaningful and rewarding.
3. **Consistent Engagement in Community:** Actively participate in community activities and groups that align with your values and interests. Sustained involvement in community life provides ongoing support, purpose, and opportunities for meaningful connection.
4. **Maintaining Balanced Relationships:** Strive for balance within your relationships, ensuring reciprocal support and emotional exchange. Healthy, balanced relationships foster long-term fulfillment and prevent emotional exhaustion or burnout.
5. **Adaptability and Flexibility:** Develop the capacity to adapt to changing social circumstances and evolving personal relationships. Flexibility helps you maintain

fulfilling connections through various life stages and transitions.
6. **Regular Reflection and Adjustment:** Regularly reflect on your social relationships, identifying areas for growth or improvement. Periodic reflection helps you proactively address issues, reinforce positive behaviors, and ensure long-term relationship satisfaction.
7. **Fostering New Connections:** Remain open to cultivating new relationships throughout life. Welcoming new connections ensures continued social growth, diversification of your social circle, and ongoing social enrichment.
8. **Prioritizing Meaningful Experiences:** Engage in meaningful, shared experiences with others that build lasting memories and emotional bonds. Prioritizing activities that deepen relationships contributes significantly to sustained social satisfaction.

Cultivating long-term social fulfillment requires intentional commitment and consistent engagement. By actively nurturing relationships, embracing growth, and prioritizing meaningful connections, you ensure sustained social well-being and fulfillment throughout your life.

Sustaining friendships over time

Maintaining friendships over time is crucial for emotional health, social stability, and personal fulfillment. While life naturally involves changes, sustaining these relationships requires intentionality, effort, and understanding. Here are practical strategies to nurture and preserve your friendships long-term:

1. **Consistent Communication:** Stay connected regularly through calls, texts, social media, or in-person meetings.

Invisible

Consistent communication reinforces emotional bonds and ensures your friendships remain vibrant and relevant.

2. **Showing Genuine Interest:** Regularly express genuine curiosity and care about your friends' lives, goals, and challenges. Demonstrating sincere interest strengthens emotional connections and trust.
3. **Practicing Empathy and Support:** Offer emotional support during difficult times and celebrate their successes and milestones. Empathy builds a strong emotional foundation, ensuring friendships endure through life's ups and downs.
4. **Maintaining Flexibility:** Understand and accept changes in your friends' lives, including shifting interests, priorities, or circumstances. Flexibility ensures your friendships remain adaptable and resilient.
5. **Prioritizing Face-to-Face Interactions:** Whenever possible, prioritize in-person meetings and activities. Face-to-face interactions deepen connections, create meaningful memories, and enrich your shared experiences.
6. **Resolving Conflicts Constructively:** Address disagreements openly, honestly, and constructively. Effectively resolving conflicts strengthens trust and demonstrates mutual respect and commitment to the friendship.
7. **Celebrating Traditions and Rituals:** Establish and maintain rituals or traditions, such as annual get-togethers, monthly dinners, or regular outings. These shared traditions build a sense of continuity, belonging, and deeper emotional bonds.
8. **Acknowledging and Appreciating:** Regularly acknowledge and appreciate your friends' presence, efforts, and contributions to your life. Small gestures of

appreciation reinforce mutual affection and sustain positive dynamics.

Sustaining friendships over time requires consistent effort, genuine care, and adaptability. By intentionally nurturing your friendships, you can build long-lasting, enriching connections that enhance your emotional well-being throughout your life.

The habits of socially fulfilled individuals

Socially fulfilled individuals tend to share certain habits that consistently contribute to their happiness, emotional stability, and relational satisfaction. Adopting these habits can significantly enhance your own social life and overall sense of well-being:

1. **Prioritizing Meaningful Interactions:** Focus on quality over quantity in relationships, investing more deeply in meaningful interactions that foster genuine connection, trust, and emotional intimacy.
2. **Practicing Gratitude Regularly:** Frequently express gratitude for relationships, experiences, and connections. Gratitude enhances positive emotions, strengthens bonds, and promotes relationship longevity.
3. **Being Proactively Social:** Actively create opportunities to engage socially, initiate conversations, and organize gatherings. Proactivity helps maintain a vibrant and fulfilling social life.
4. **Maintaining Emotional Openness:** Cultivate openness and vulnerability in relationships. Sharing authentic emotions and experiences allows for deeper connections and trust.
5. **Balancing Social Time with Personal Time:** Regularly balance social activities with personal time for

self-care and reflection. This balance helps sustain emotional health, preventing social burnout.
6. **Consistent Acts of Kindness:** Regularly perform acts of kindness and thoughtful gestures towards friends, family, and community. Kindness reinforces connections, creates positive interactions, and nurtures emotional fulfillment.
7. **Continuous Learning and Growth:** Embrace lifelong learning and personal growth. Socially fulfilled individuals remain curious, exploring new interests and experiences that facilitate fresh connections and enrich existing relationships.
8. **Effective Communication:** Develop and maintain clear, empathetic, and effective communication skills. Being an attentive listener and thoughtful communicator strengthens trust, respect, and mutual understanding.

Incorporating these habits into your daily life can significantly enhance your social fulfillment, deepen relationships, and foster a more emotionally satisfying and socially connected life.

Continuously evolving your social life to fit your needs

Your social life should continuously evolve alongside your personal growth, changing circumstances, and shifting needs. Being adaptable and responsive to your evolving social needs ensures sustained happiness, emotional balance, and fulfillment. Consider these strategies to continuously evolve and enrich your social interactions:

1. **Regular Self-Assessment:** Periodically reflect on your current social needs, preferences, and satisfaction levels.

Honest self-assessment helps you recognize changes early and adapt proactively.
2. **Staying Open to New Experiences:** Maintain openness to exploring new interests, activities, and social opportunities. Embracing new experiences keeps your social life vibrant, engaging, and fulfilling.
3. **Cultivating Adaptability:** Develop the ability to adapt comfortably to changing situations, relationships, and interests. Flexibility allows you to embrace change positively, enriching your social experiences.
4. **Mindfully Managing Transitions:** Approach life transitions mindfully, recognizing them as opportunities to reassess and recalibrate your social connections and goals. Effective management of transitions ensures continued growth and satisfaction.
5. **Proactive Communication:** Clearly and openly communicate your changing needs and expectations to friends and social circles. Honest communication fosters understanding and supports mutual adaptation.
6. **Seeking Continuous Learning:** Pursue continuous learning and personal development, enhancing your interpersonal skills, emotional intelligence, and self-awareness. Lifelong learning facilitates deeper, more meaningful social connections.
7. **Balancing Consistency with Novelty:** Balance regular, comforting social routines with occasional novel experiences. This approach ensures both stability and excitement in your social life.
8. **Nurturing Diverse Relationships:** Cultivate a diverse range of relationships, ensuring your social circle includes varied perspectives, experiences, and interests. Diversity in relationships contributes significantly to ongoing personal growth and social enrichment.

Invisible

By continuously evolving your social life to fit your changing needs, you create a dynamic, fulfilling, and deeply satisfying social experience throughout your lifetime.

Anissa Brodon

Self-Reflection: Cultivating Long-Term Social Fulfillment

1. **What does social fulfillment mean to me personally?**
   Is it about depth, consistency, laughter, purpose, or being understood?

2. **Which relationships in my life feel the most nourishing and long-lasting?**
   What makes them that way?

3. **Have I been intentional in how I build and maintain my social circle—or mostly reactive?**

4. **Am I investing in people who invest in me in return?**
   Where is the balance of energy and effort?

5. **What do I need in a long-term friendship or community to feel emotionally safe and seen?**

6. **Do I make space for both giving and receiving support?**
   Or do I tend to lean more heavily in one direction?

7. **What habits or patterns help me keep relationships strong over time?**
   (e.g., regular check-ins, honesty, shared rituals, vulnerability)

8. **Have I communicated my needs and values clearly in my closest relationships?**
   What could I be more honest about?

9. **What role does forgiveness, growth, or adaptability play in my long-term connections?**
   How have these helped me maintain or rebuild bonds?

10. **Do I allow room for friendships to evolve—or do I expect them to stay the same?**

11. **What have I learned from past relationships that I want to apply moving forward?**

12. **Am I open to deepening current relationships—not just seeking new ones?**

13. **Do I prioritize time for connection in the same way I prioritize work, health, or goals?**

14. **What fears or blocks might be holding me back from fully opening up or committing to long-term friendships?**

15. **What small, regular actions can I take to cultivate joy, trust, and meaning in my social life—for years to come?**

Invisible

Anissa Brodon

Chapter 11: Becoming Visible Again

Reclaiming visibility in your social life after 40 is a powerful journey toward emotional fulfillment, personal growth, and lasting happiness. As you have navigated through the complexities and barriers discussed throughout this book, you now have the tools, strategies, and insights needed to reconnect deeply and authentically with others.

Embracing your visibility involves understanding your inherent worth, rediscovering your confidence, and actively nurturing meaningful relationships. It requires both courage and intention—courage to step beyond comfort zones, and intention to continually adapt and evolve socially.

Visibility is not simply about being seen by others but also about feeling deeply understood, appreciated, and valued. By applying the lessons and practices you've explored, you can build vibrant social circles that support your well-being, celebrate your authenticity, and encourage your growth.

Moving forward, commit to remaining proactive, open-minded, and adaptable. Cultivate ongoing self-awareness, practice compassionate communication, and embrace continuous learning and growth. Your social journey is dynamic, ever-changing, and filled with potential for deep fulfillment.

You deserve to be seen, heard, and cherished. Step boldly into your social visibility, confident in the knowledge that meaningful connections and enriching relationships await you. Welcome back to visibility—embrace the richness and joy that comes from being fully and authentically connected to the world around you.

Recap of strategies for rebuilding and maintaining social visibility

Throughout this book, we've explored various strategies to help you rebuild and sustain your social visibility, enhancing your emotional and relational well-being. Here's a concise recap to guide your ongoing journey:

1. **Understand Your Social Needs:** Regularly reflect on your personal needs and desires in relationships to ensure alignment with your evolving identity.
2. **Build and Maintain Confidence:** Cultivate social confidence through practice, positive self-talk, and recognizing your inherent worth.
3. **Reconnect and Reinforce:** Proactively rebuild old friendships and actively nurture existing bonds through consistent communication and genuine engagement.
4. **Create New Connections:** Employ practical strategies to form new friendships, including joining interest-based groups and leveraging shared hobbies.
5. **Embrace Community:** Engage actively with communities—local, online, or interest-based—to enhance belonging and mutual support.
6. **Maintain Healthy Boundaries:** Clearly establish and communicate your boundaries to foster respectful and balanced interactions.
7. **Adapt to Life Transitions:** View significant life changes as opportunities to redefine yourself socially, remaining flexible and proactive during these periods.
8. **Leverage Technology:** Utilize social media and online platforms to widen your social circle and deepen existing connections.

9. **Navigate Social Dynamics:** Develop strategies to effectively manage difficult interactions, conflicts, and changing circumstances.
10. **Balance Intimacy and Independence:** Achieve a harmonious balance between close personal relationships, independent pursuits, and community involvement.
11. **Continuous Growth and Evolution:** Stay open to ongoing learning, adapting your social life as your needs and circumstances change.

Applying these strategies consistently will allow you to rebuild your social visibility, creating meaningful, fulfilling relationships that enrich your life profoundly.

Anissa Brodon

Self-Reflection: Becoming Visible Again

1. **When did I start to feel invisible—and what was happening in my life at that time?**
   Was it gradual or tied to a specific event or role?

2. **What parts of myself have I hidden, quieted, or set aside for the sake of others?**
   Why did I feel the need to do that?

3. **Who was I before I felt invisible?**
   What words, traits, or dreams describe that version of me?

4. **What do I miss most about being seen, heard, and valued?**
   What does "visibility" mean to me now?

5. **Have I internalized the belief that I need to stay small, quiet, or in the background?**
   Where did that belief come from—and is it still true?

6. **In what spaces or relationships do I still feel unseen or overlooked?**
   What would I say or do if I felt fully empowered?

7. **How have I learned to minimize myself to avoid judgment, conflict, or rejection?**

8. **What does being "visible" look like for me today—not for attention, but for authenticity?**

9. **What makes me feel most alive and expressive?**
   How often do I make space for that?

10. **Am I allowing myself to take up emotional, creative, or physical space?**
    Where am I still holding back?

11. **How do I want to reintroduce myself to the world?**
    What would I want people to know or see?

12. **What fears or vulnerabilities come up when I think about stepping into the spotlight again?**

13. **What support or encouragement do I need to feel safe being seen again?**
    Who can I reach out to?

14. **What small act of visibility can I take today—just for me?**
    (e.g., speaking up, wearing something bold, sharing my story, setting a boundary)

15. **What truth about myself am I ready to embrace—and no longer apologize for?**

Epilogue

Living a connected and fulfilling social life after 40 is not only possible—it's a powerful expression of self-worth, courage, and renewal. The journey of becoming socially visible again is about reclaiming your presence in the world, reigniting your passions, and building connections that reflect who you truly are.

This stage of life offers a unique gift: the wisdom of experience combined with the freedom to choose who you want to be. You are not defined by past social roles, relationships, or perceived limitations. Instead, you are empowered to shape a life rich in connection, authenticity, and joy.

Let this be a call to action—to reach out, speak up, and step forward. Take that class. Send that message. Attend that gathering. Create space for laughter, vulnerability, and shared experience. Even small steps can open doors to extraordinary friendships and transformative community.

Remember, connection begins with intention. Whether you're rebuilding, redefining, or just beginning again, know that every effort to connect is a powerful affirmation of your worth.

You are not alone.

You are still becoming.

And your most fulfilling, connected life can start right now.

Anissa Brodon

Appendix A

Resources for further reading

Books
- *Friendships Don't Just Happen!* by Shasta Nelson
  A practical guide for women looking to cultivate meaningful female friendships in adulthood.
- *Frientimacy* by Shasta Nelson
  Focuses on deepening existing friendships and understanding emotional intimacy in adult relationships.
- *Platonic: How the Science of Attachment Can Help You Make—and Keep—Friends* by Marisa G. Franco, PhD
  Blends science and storytelling to explore how we form and sustain adult friendships.
- *The Friendship Formula* by Caroline Millington
  Offers easy-to-follow guidance and real-life stories to help improve your friendship landscape at any age.

Websites & Articles
- Psychology Today (www.psychologytoday.com): Search for articles on "adult friendship" and "making friends after 40."
- The Gottman Institute (www.gottman.com): Features science-backed insights into emotional connection and relationship building.
- TED Talks:
  - "The secret to making new friends as an adult" by Marisa Franco
  - "What makes a good life? Lessons from the longest study on happiness" by Robert Waldinger

Anissa Brodon

Online Communities & Platforms
- **Meetup.com** – Find or start local groups based on shared interests.
- **Nextdoor** – Connect with neighbors and discover local events.
- **Bumble BFF** – A friend-finding feature in the Bumble app tailored to building platonic relationships.
- **Facebook Groups** – Search for local or themed groups that match your hobbies or life stage.

Workshops & Support Groups
- Local community centers, YMCAs, libraries, and adult learning centers often offer social and interest-based programs.
- Therapy groups or life coaching programs can provide guided support in building confidence and social skills.

Invisible

Anissa Brodon

Appendix B

Worksheets and Self-Assessment Tools

Friendship Inventory Worksheet
- Who are my closest friends right now?
- How often do I connect with them?
- What qualities do I value in a friend?

Social Needs Self-Assessment
- Do I prefer one-on-one connections or group settings?
- What types of interactions energize me?
- How do I feel after socializing?

Connection Goals Planner
- One person I want to reconnect with this month is: _____
- One new activity I'd like to try to meet new people: _____
- My weekly social time goal: _____ hours

Confidence Reflection Sheet
- A time I felt socially confident: _____
- What helped me feel that way?
- One affirmation I can say before social events: _____

Boundary Setting Prompts
- What are my emotional and social limits?
- How can I kindly communicate my needs?
- How do I recognize when a boundary is being crossed?

Anissa Brodon

Appendix C: Journal Prompts for Personal Reflection

- What does social connection mean to me at this stage in life?
- When do I feel most seen and understood by others?
- How have my relationships changed over the years, and what have I learned from those changes?
- What kind of people do I feel drawn to now, and why?
- What are my fears about reaching out socially—and where do those fears come from?
- What role do I want to play in my community or social circles?
- How do I recharge best after socializing, and how can I honor that need?
- What past social experience would I like to reframe or heal from?
- What does being "visible" mean to me?
- How can I commit to nurturing my social life moving forward?

These prompts are designed to encourage deep reflection and help clarify your values, motivations, and aspirations for a more connected, authentic life.

Printed in Great Britain
by Amazon

3bc289ed-187b-4c6e-9545-dff77fe2abd8R01